Angelology

A STUDY ON THE SECRET MESSENGERS OF GOD

BY

KEN CHANT

Angelology

A STUDY ON THE SECRET MESSENGERS OF GOD

BY

KEN CHANT

Copyright © 2012 by Ken Chant

ISBN 978-1-61529-037-0

Vision Publishing
1672 Main St. E 109
Ramona, CA 92065
1-800-9-VISION
www.booksbyvision.com

A NOTE ON GENDER

It is unfortunate that the English language does not contain an adequate generic pronoun (especially in the singular number) that includes without bias both male and female. So *"he, him, his, man, mankind,"* with their plurals, must do the work for both sexes. Accordingly, wherever it is appropriate to do so in the following pages, please include the feminine gender in the masculine, and vice versa.

FOOTNOTES

A work once fully referenced will thereafter be noted either by "ibid" or "op. cit."

CONTENTS

ABBREVIATIONS

Abbreviations commonly used for the books of the Bible are

Genesis	Ge	Habakkuk	Hb
Exodus	Ex	Zephaniah	Zp
Leviticus	Le	Haggai	Hg
Numbers	Nu	Zechariah	Zc
Deuteronomy	De	Malachi	Mal
Joshua	Js		
Judges	Jg		
Ruth	Ru	Matthew	Mt
1 Samuel	1 Sa	Mark	Mk
2 Samuel	2 Sa	Luke	Lu
1 Kings	1 Kg	John	Jn
2 Kings	2 Kg	Acts	Ac
1 Chronicles	1 Ch	Romans	Ro
2 Chronicles	2 Ch	1 Corinthians	1 Co
Ezra	Ezr	2 Corinthians	2 Co
Nehemiah	Ne	Galatians	Ga
Esther	Es	Ephesians	Ep
Job	Jb	Philippians	Ph
Psalm	Ps	Colossians	Cl
Proverbs	Pr	1 Thessalonians	1 Th
Ecclesiastes	Ec	2 Thessalonians	2 Th
Song of Songs	Ca *	1 Timothy	1 Ti
Isaiah	Is	2 Timothy	2 Ti
Jeremiah	Je	Titus	Tit
Lamentations	La	Philemon	Phm
Ezekiel	Ez	Hebrews	He
Daniel	Da	James	Ja
Hosea	Ho	1 Peter	1 Pe
Joel	Jl	2 Peter	2 Pe
Amos	Am	1 John	1 Jn
Obadiah	Ob	2 John	2 Jn
Jonah	Jo	3 John	3 Jn
Micah	Mi	Jude	Ju
Nahum	Na	Revelation	Re

Ca is an abbreviation of *Canticles*, a derivative of the Latin name of the *Song of Solomon*, which is sometimes also called the *Song of Songs*.

A WORLD OF WONDER

You are about to begin a fascinating adventure: a quest to penetrate the veil, to step into another dimension, to learn what is happening in the world of spirits.

Our quest is in two sections, the first (this book) deals with the kingdom of light, and the second (my book *Demonology)* with the kingdom of darkness. You will find familiar things here; you may also find things that startle and amaze you. Unless you are already full of knowledge, I am sure the following pages will enrich your understanding of the place occupied by angels and demons in God's world. Even well-informed students may find themselves encountering here some new ideas, some new ways of looking at the realm of both good and evil spirits.

You will find no anecdotes about angels or demons, except those that come out of the Bible. I have refrained from building doctrine either on my own experiences or those of others. Other books that I have read about the subject abound in such stories, but I find many of them unconvincing.

The devil and demons entice some writers to present as normal and necessary quite sensational behaviour and quite speculative notions. I am certain many of those conjectures are spurious, and much of the erratic behaviour reported by some authors is merely psychic. I have grave doubts even about some of the things I have observed in my own ministry of exorcism, let alone what I have seen in the ministry of others. So I resolved in these pages to avoid personal testimony, and to stick to scripture.

I regret having had more discernible contact over the years with demons than with angels - yet I am confident the holy angels have been continually and effectively active in my life, and I hope what I have written will show this, along with the honour and gratitude I feel toward them.

Writing these two books has reinforced my belief that it is unwise to desire too much knowledge about either angels or demons. We should be content with what scripture tells us. To yearn for more is perilous, and may lead to deep deception. These pages will serve you well if they do no more (nor any less) than sufficiently expose you to the world of angels to enhance your confidence in God, and to the world of demons to ensure your personal mastery over Satan and all his works.

For the rest, Henry David Thoreau's admonition may serve us all well -

> Most people with whom I talk, men and women even of some originality and genius, have their scheme of the universe all cut and dried - very dry, I assure you, to hear, dry enough to burn, dry-rotted and powder-post, methinks - which they set up between you and them in the shortest intercourse; an ancient and tottering frame with all its boards blown off ... The wisest man preaches no doctrines; he has no scheme; he sees no rafter, not even a cobweb against the heavens. It is a clear sky ... (Yet your) scheme must be the framework of the universe; all other schemes will soon be ruins. The perfect God in his revelation of himself has never got to the length of one such proposition as you, his prophets, state. Have you learned the alphabet of heaven and can count three? Do you know the number of God's family? Can you put mysteries into words? Do you presume to fable the ineffable? Pray, what geographers are you that speak of heaven's topography? Whose friend are you that speak of God's personality? ... Tell me of the height of the mountains of the moon, or of the diameter of space,

and I may believe you; but of the secret history of
the Almighty, and I shall pronounce you mad.[1]

Thoreau was a little cavalier in his dismissal of all dogma. It is foolish to reckon that no certainty about anything is possible. But he was true enough in rejecting those mad prophets who are certain about everything! Some honest ignorance will do us no harm. Moses had a good balance -

The secret things belong to the Lord our God, but the things revealed belong to us and to our children for ever *(De 29:29)*

Let God keep secret what he pleases; let us be content with what he reveals.

DID YOU MEET AN ANGEL TODAY?

Jacob went on his way and the angels of God met him; and when he saw them he said, "This is God's army!" So he called the name of the place "Mahanaim" - "The Two Armies!" *(Ge 32:1-2)*

You are setting out on your journey into tomorrow. What will you meet? If your way is God's way, and you have the right eyes, the first thing you will see coming to meet you out of the unknown will be God's mighty host! You will be able to laugh with Jacob, "Two armies! I and the angels of the Almighty!"

Of course, that will mean nothing to you if you do not believe in angels. But if that is the case, and unless you are willing to change your mind, you may as well discard these chapters right now. For

---

[1] A Week On The Concord And Merrimack Rivers; The Heritage Press, Norwalk CT, 1975; pg 55,56 ("Sunday"). This book appeared in 1849 and was the first of the only two of his books that were published in his lifetime (the other was WALDEN). Both books are extraordinary in the idyllic serenity, penetrating observation, and literary power, and since Thoreau's death they have had far-flung influence. His *Week* sold only about 300 of 1000 copies that were printed. It is said the Thoreau observed ruefully that he had somewhat more than a thousand books in his library, of which seven hundred were written by himself!

we are not like the Sadducees (Ac 23:8), we do believe everything the Bible tells us about the angels. We expect that shining host of heavenly messengers to be as much at work today as ever they have been in the past. Although it may be *"unawares"* (He 13:2), we have no doubt the servants of God today may just as readily meet with an angel as ever Jacob of old did.

Who the angels are, what they do, and what your relationship with them should be, are the themes of this book. But before we begin, let these promises of God whet your anticipation -

The angel of the Lord encamps around those who fear him, and delivers them! (Ps 34:7)

He will give his angels charge of you, to guard you in all your ways. On their hands they will bear you up, lest you dash your foot against a stone. *(Ps 91:11-12)*

See that you do not despise one of these little ones; for I tell you that in heaven their angels always behold the face of my Father who is in heaven *(Mt 18:10)*

Are the angels not all ministering spirits sent forth to serve, for the sake of those who are to obtain salvation? *(He 1:14)*

I believe the angels are still doing just what they did in Bible days: guiding, revealing, warning, instructing, protecting, helping.

CHAPTER ONE

ANGELS,
ANCIENT AND MODERN

The ancients were fascinated by angels. All kinds of arcane angelic lore became the subject of enthusiastic and heated debate. Those grave scholars zealously argued about how many angels could stand on the point of a pin, or whether an angel could be in two places at one time - topics that were not as frivolous as they may at first seem, for they dealt with the relation of angels to space.

The savants also wondered: do angels have a specific size, or can they expand and contract themselves? Are they wholly spirit-beings, or do they have some substance? Perhaps they are merely mobile intelligences, not having any form? Perhaps they have bodies composed of some ethereal matter, malleable, and able to assume any required shape, visible or invisible? Since they apparently have knowledge of many things, is this knowledge based on observation, reasoning, and argument (like man's), or does it arise from immediate intuition? Can angels "feel", or are they wholly dispassionate?

The endless and fervent debates continued. How great was the interval between the creation of the angels and their fall? Did the sin of the first angel cause the sin of the rest, or did each corrupt angel fall in proud isolation? How many of the angels fell, and how many retained their integrity? Is our atmosphere the place of punishment for fallen angels? Do guardian angels have charge of children from baptism, from birth, or while the infant is yet in the womb of its mother?

Even those questions did not satisfy them. Still they pondered: how many are the angels; what are their names; what ranks do they have? Are some of them guardians of nations, cities, communities, or individuals? Is God creating more angels, or is their number fixed? Will the righteous become angels? Do angels carry our prayers into heaven? And so on, and on!

A. H. Strong says that "even the excrements of angels were subjects of discussion, for if there was 'angel's food' (Ps 78:25), and if angels ate (Ge 18:8), it was argued that we must take the logical consequences."[1]

Even the Koran reports Allah as saying with a perplexing ambiguity -

> (Hell) is guarded by nineteen keepers. We have appointed none but angels to guard the Fire, and made their number a subject for dispute among the unbelievers, so that those to whom the Scriptures were given may be convinced, and the true believers strengthened in their faith ... and that the infidels and hypocrites may say: "What could Allah mean by this?" Thus Allah misleads whom he will and guides whom he pleases. None knows the warriors of your Lord but Himself.[3]

Mohammed seems there to keep his coin while spending it. He says there are nineteen angels guarding the Fire of perdition, but then mocks both his own number and those who debate such matters. Are there nineteen? Or is that just a fiction intended to mire infidels in futile disputes? Is the number real or symbolic? Perhaps it is only divine trickery, since no one but God knows "the warriors" of heaven! At least it shows an exasperation with the endless arguments of the Jewish and Christian divines!

---

[2]   Systematic Theology, pg. 443; Pickering & Inglis Ltd., London, 1907.

[3]   The Koran, Sura 74:31, tr. N. J. Dawood; Penguin Books, London, 1980; pg. 56.

FOUR INFLUENTIAL STREAMS

The four great Western religions (Judaism, Zoroastrianism, Christianity, and Islam) have all believed in angels. They mostly agree that angels are obedient servants of God, and that they are ranked in a hierarchy of importance, function, and power.

The basis of that common belief was probably an instinctive assumption that there must be a correspondence between the structures of earthly kingdoms and the kingdom of heaven. If God is a King, then surely he rules a kingdom, and echelons of princes, courtiers, and other authorities, must surround his throne. We are going to look at three of the four great religions, beginning with

A. Judaism

The Old Testament contains little definition of the heavenly realm, which shows that the ancient Israelites probably had only vague images of the nature and functions of angels. But after Cyrus made himself master of Palestine, Persian mythology began to exercise a profound influence upon Jewish beliefs. Some of that mythology happened to be true, and Christ endorsed it. So also did the apostles. But much of it was spurious.

1. The Seven Angels - And More!

The rabbis were enthusiastic in their speculations about the angels. They divided the heavenly host into many orders and ranks, and found names for at least seven archangels:

- Uriel   commander of the battalions, and governor of Sheol

- Raphael   bringer of healing, and protector of souls

- Raguel   wreaker of divine vengeance

- Michael   mighty warrior of Israel

- Sariel   avenger of the spirits

- ♦ Gabriel   special messenger of God, and ruler of Paradise

- ♦ Remiel   keeper of the souls in Sheol/Hades.

One ancient work, still extant, *The Book Of Enoch*, cites the names of about 150 angels! Here are some of them -

> There are seven great, beautiful, wonderful, and honoured princes who are in charge of the seven heavens. They are Michael, Gabriel, Satqi'el, Sahaqi'el, Baradi'el, Baraqi'el, and Sidri'el. Each of them is a prince over a heavenly host, and every one of them is attended by 496,000 myriads of ministering angels ... Under them is Galgalli'el, the Prince, who is in charge of the orb of the sun, and with him are 96 angels, mighty and honoured ... Above them is a prince, noble, wonderful, mighty, praised with all manner of praise: Kerubi'el ... a valiant prince, full of boundless power; a majestic prince ... a prince glorified by thousands of hosts, a prince extolled by countless legions. At his wrath the earth quakes ... His body is full of burning coals; it is as high as the seven heavens, as broad as the seven heavens, as wide as the seven heavens ...[4]

> - ♦ The rabbis claimed that one vast angel, Sandalfon, was "taller than his fellows by the length of a journey of 500 years"; and they had a marvellous array of sayings about the huge dimensions of other angels. They argued about the number of the angels; their connection with

---

[4] The Hebrew *Apocalypse of Enoch*, an anonymous 5th - 6th century A.D. Jewish work, based on older traditions; ch. 17 & 22. From <u>The Old Testament Pseudepigrapha</u>, Vol. One; ed. J. H. Charlesworth; Doubleday & Co, New York; 1985; pg. 269, 277.

"the four elements"; whether they took material bodies when they appeared to men, or merely seemed to do so; how many gradations of angels there are; does God still create angels; do the righteous turn into angels; are angels jealous of man; and the like.

♦ The sages placed particular emphasis upon the role of angels as mediators between God and man. They taught that one of the great functions of angels was to carry the prayers of the saints into the throne room of God, and to present these petitions to the mighty King. They delighted to think the Shining Ones were interceding for them, face to face with God. They talked about the great receptacle into which the prayers of the saints were placed, so that Michael could carry them through the golden doors and into the presence of the God of glory.

♦ Mention is made of the seven in Tobit 12:15, "I am Raphael, one of the seven angels who stand ever ready to enter the presence of the glory of the Lord." The vision of John *echoes the same belief -*

John, to the seven churches that are in Asia ... To the angel of the church in Ephesus write ... (Re 1:4 & 2:1)

The words of him who has the seven spirits of God, and the seven stars. (Re 3:1)

Before the throne burn seven torches of fire, which are the seven spirits of God. (Re 4:5)

> *... with seven eyes, which are the seven spirits of God sent out into all the earth. (Re 5:6).*
>
> *These seven angels, or spirits, were a traditional part of Jewish angelology. Tobit calls them Angels of the Presence, an idea that is also echoed in the Apocalypse -*
>
> *I saw the seven angels who stand before God, and seven trumpets were given to them. (Re 8:2)*
>
> *Then I saw seven angels with seven plagues, which are the last, for with them the wrath of God is ended. (Re 15:1).*

In the idiom of the day, the expressions *of the Presence*, and *before the Throne*, carried the idea of "chosen by God to be his special servants" - in other words, it was a designation of rank, or authority, rather than of fixed position.

Some of the early Christians were prone to adopt the Jewish traditions without question. Many of the church Fathers also accepted *Tobit* as scripture (as Roman Catholics and others still do). Thus they added Raphael to the biblically named Michael and Gabriel. For example, Origen wrote,

> To Raphael (was given) the work of curing and healing; to Gabriel, the conduct of wars; to Michael, the duty of attending to the prayers and supplications of mortals.[5]

Likewise, early Christians often placed between themselves and God an almost endless series of spirit-beings, each ranked a little higher than the other; nor did they hesitate to pray to these angels, and to seek their mediation in heaven. Paul vigorously argued against such folly in his letter to the Colossians. He insisted we all have open

---

[5]   On The Principles, Bk 1, ch 8; written circa 215.

access to God through Christ; hence we have no need of angels to bring us into the Father's presence - see Cl 1:15-19; 2:4, 8-10, 18-20.

2. NAMING THE ANGELS

The urge to name the angels probably had its roots in pagan superstition. The belief was (and among some people still is) widespread that knowing the name of a spirit-being gives one power over it, or at least the right to invoke its aid. The Christian apologist Arnobius (circa 300) referred to that ancient superstition -

> My opponent will perhaps meet me with many other slanderous and childish charges, which are commonly urged. Such as: Jesus was a magician; he effected all (his miracles) by secret arts; from the shrines of the Egyptians he stole the names of the angels of might ... Why, O witlings, do you speak of things which you have not examined ... ? Were then those things that were done the freaks of demons and the tricks of magical arts? Can you specify ... any one of all those magicians who have ever existed in past ages that did anything similar, in the thousandth degree, to Christ?[6]

The Egyptians cast fear upon the ancient world because the priests (so it was said) had a secret knowledge of demonic names. That magical lore gave them an awful esoteric power. They could bend the forces of darkness to their own will. How could mere flesh resist such invisible strength? People began to whisper the same about Jesus. Had he not spent part of his childhood in Egypt? Perhaps somehow he had uncovered the secrets of the magicians? That is why (they shuddered) he could compel spirits to do his bidding! How else could he have such power over demons? Arnobius rightly mocked such silly delusions.

---

[6]   Against The Heathen; par. 43.

The famed historian Josephus presents a similar idea (*Wars 2.8.7*), in a passage dealing with the conditions the Essenes imposed upon applicants to their order -

> ... and before he is allowed to touch their common food, he is obliged to take tremendous oaths ... that he will equally preserve the books belonging to their sect, and the names of the angels. These are the oaths by which they secure their proselytes to themselves.

Along with other Jewish mystics of the period, the Essenes apparently believed that the revelations they had received were a special sign of divine favour. Their arcane lore about the names of angels proved their election as God's chosen people. Those names were also a source of occult power. They gave the Essenes mastery over the world of spirits. The angels (it was believed) had no choice but to do the will of those who could name them.

But where did the names come from? The Hebrew or Greek words for "God", linked with various noble adjectives, provided many angelic names. An example is Gabri-el, which means God-Is-Great. Others arose from a particular task the angel was supposed to perform, such as Raphael, which means Divine Healer. Still others were constructed by using different combinations of "magical" letters and numbers - some of the names in The Book Of Enoch (mentioned above) display those superstitious patterns.[7] Some were no doubt pure inventions. Some probably came out of glossolalic utterances - a phenomenon encountered among a few modern pentecostals. I have had people come to me with lists of angelic names they claimed God revealed to them as they spoke in tongues; and you can find the same in some charismatic paperbacks.

---

[7] The Old Testament Pseudepigrapha, Vol. Two; pg. 55

The apostles derided such speculations. They resisted superstitious fancies. Cautious restraint marks their comments on the angels. Even the Apocalypse, despite its colourful hyperbole, avoids the wild excesses of contemporary writers. In scripture, the angels are mostly anonymous, and they prefer to remain that way (cp. Jg 13:18). I am instantly suspicious of the claims of any person, whether Christian or pagan, that angels have appeared to them and disclosed their names. Nor is there any good reason to give any more credence to modern names inspired by glossolalia than to ancient ones. Despite the hunger of some people to know the names and number of angels, only two are identified in the Bible: Michael, and Gabriel (both of whom are mentioned in both Testaments.) Beyond those two, there is only worthless speculation.

3. Rabbinical Traditions

a. The Nine Choirs

An early Jewish belief (taught in *The Book Of Jubilees*, circa 150 B.C.) was that there are eight gradations of angels -

> For on the first day he created the heavens ... (and then) all of the spirits that minister before him:
>
> *the angels of the presence,*
>
> *and the angels of sanctification,*
>
> *and the angels of the spirit of fire,*
>
> *and the angels of the spirit of the winds,*
>
> *and the angels of the spirit of the clouds,*
>
> *and darkness and snow and hail and frost,*
>
> *and the angels of resoundings and thunder and lightnings,*
>
> *and the angels of the spirits of cold and heat*

and winter and springtime and harvest and summer,

and all of the spirits of his creatures

which are in heaven and on earth.

... Then we saw his works and blessed him and
offered praise before him on account of all his
works ... (2:2).[8]

Those eight grades were then divided into three classes: *Angels of
the Presence; Angels of Sanctification* (including guardian angels);
and an inferior class of *Nature Angels*, set over the forces of nature.
Jubilees 15:27 suggests those categories -

Because the nature of all of the angels of the
presence and all of the angels of sanctification was
thus from the day of their creation. And in the
presence of the angels of the presence and the
angels of sanctification he sanctified Israel so that
they might be with him and with his holy angels.[9]

Others posited four, seven, twelve, or even more ranks of angels. In
popular thought, the number of ranks in the hierarchy was
sometimes linked with the number of tiers in an oriental monarchy,
or with the number of the planetary spheres, or with some other
parallel structure. A common grouping, which although based on
OT data remains quite arbitrary, was -

♦ archangels

♦ seraphim

♦ cherubim

[8] Op. cit. The translator, P. Alexander, gives an example: "A case in point is
'Azbogah (Enoch 18:2). This name is made up of three pairs of consonants, each of
which adds up by gematria to eight." (Pg. 24)

[9] Ibid., pg. 87

- ophanim ("wheels", Ez 1:15; etc)
- powers
- principalities
- holy ones
- lordships.

Under the influence of such Jewish ideas, the medieval church finally settled upon the classification of the angels into the famous "nine choirs" composed of three companies -

i. Counsellors

seraphim, cherubim, thrones: who stand in perpetual adoration around the throne of God and radiate the glory of God.

ii. Governors

dominions, virtues, powers: who receive divine illumination from the first hierarchy and communicate it to the third, but remain aloof from mortals.

iii. Messengers

principalities, archangels, angels: who intervene in the affairs of mankind.[10]

There is scant reason to accept any of those arbitrary and fanciful compilations, whether Jewish or Christian.

b. Nature Angels

Some rabbis adapted pagan mythology to their own use, and taught that the sun, moon, stars, the passage of the seasons, and the like, were all controlled by angels. Each part of nature, each element of the physical realm, had its heavenly counterpart. The task of the

---

[10] Dictionary Of Christian Lore And Legend, ed. J. C. J. Metford; Thames & Hudson, London, 1983; pg. 26.

angels, so the Jewish sages claimed, was to be the agents of God's providence, to guard and control the material world.

That view, too, was popular in the early church. Origen wrote -

> Angels are set over the fruits of the earth, and over the birth of animals.[11]

And Athenagoras taught (circa 180) -

> The angels were created by God and entrusted with the control of matter ... For this is the office of angels, to exercise the providence of God over the things ordered and created by him; so that God may have universal and general providence of the whole, while the particular parts are provided by the angels that are appointed over each of them.[12]

And the 5th-century Book Of Enoch, with its usual extravagance, asserts -

These are the names of the princes who guide the world:

Gabriel, the angel of fire;

Baradi'el, the angel of hail;

Ruhi'el, who is in charge of wind;

Baraqi'el, who is in charge of lightning;

Za`ami'el, who is in charge of whirlwind;

Ziqi'el, who is in charge of comets;

Zi`i'el, who is in charge of tremors;

Za`api'el, who is in charge of earthquakes

---

[11]   I have lost the source of this quote.

[12]   A Plea For Christians, ch. 24.

There may be some truth in the tradition of nature angels, for it appears to be echoed in several NT references -

♦ because the angels were thought by the Jews to be the guardians of the natural world and of its good order, therefore respect for them, and for their imminence to mankind, should cause men and women to maintain the same good order in their homes and in the church. That appears to be the reasoning behind Paul's words in 1 Co 11:10, "That is why a woman should have a veil on her head, because of the angels." Indeed, from that passage some of the Fathers concluded that the angels are intimately present at, and participate in, Christian worship.[13]

♦ the notion of particular angels having control over specific parts of the natural world is also reflected in Re 7:1; 14:18; 16:1-5 (notice the phrase in verse 5, the angel of the waters).

c. How Many Angels?

Another Jewish view adopted by at least some early Christians described the number of angels as equal to the number of human beings -

> Again I said, "Lord, how great is the multitude of angels; and which is greater, the number of angels, or of men?" And I heard a voice saying to me: "As great as is the multitude of the angels, so great is the race of men; as the prophet has said, *'He set bounds to the nations, according to the number of the angels of God.'*"[14]

---

[13] Ch. 14; op. cit., pg. 267.

[14] Thus Chrysostom, commenting on 1 Co 11:10 - "For although thou despise thy husband ... yet reverence the angels."

d. Between God and Man

The idea of angels as distinct persons who carry out divine missions upon the earth came to the fore in Jewish thinking mainly after the Exile. Part of the reason, as I have already mentioned, was the strong influence of Persian mythology; but another reason, perhaps more dominant, was a tendency to emphasise God's transcendence. The Jews had come to feel it necessary to interpose some mediaries between themselves and the awesome Deity who had so pitilessly forced the ruin of their temple and nation (cp. Jeremiah's *Lamentations*). They no longer wanted to have any close or personal encounter with the Lord. It seemed unsafe to do so. It were better to keep him distant. Notice how the following verses reflect an unconscious feeling that God should not act directly, but rather through an angelic intermediary -

> Judas prayed in these words: "There was a king whose followers blasphemed, and thy angel came forth and struck down one hundred and eighty-five thousand of them. So do thou crush this army before us today" (1 Macc 7:41).

> ... all the people, wailing and weeping, prayed for the Lord to send a good angel to deliver Israel (2 Macc 11:6).

> This was his prayer: "Master, thou didst send thy angel in the days of Hezekiah king of Judah, and he killed as many as a hundred and eighty-five thousand men in Sennacherib's camp. Now, Ruler of heaven, send once again a good angel to go in front of us spreading fear and panic" (2 Macc 15:22-23).

Does that concept of divine transcendence, of angels standing between us and the Majesty on High, have any value for the church? After all, have we not come into sweet union with the Father through Christ? That is true. Nonetheless, the doctrine of angels perhaps remains necessary to prevent us from becoming too familiar with, or contemptuous of, the Lord God. Remember that the closing book of the NT is the Apocalypse, which ardently portrays the utter glory of God, and constantly depicts angels intervening between heaven and earth.

e. Biblical Views

Other Jewish doctrines about the angels are better supported by scripture, and I will present them below simply as biblical teaching.

B. ISLAM

Muslim beliefs about angels can be summarised thus -

1. Gabriel gave Mohammed the Koran.

2. Allah is surrounded by angels, all of whom have specific duties to perform.

3. Four archangels rank above all others: Gabriel, who is Allah's messenger of inspiration; Michael, who is guardian of the Jews; Israfil, who summons the faithful at the Day of Judgment; and Isra'il, who is the Messenger of Death.

4. The angels are made of light. They do not eat or drink. (These two ideas were popular among some of the Church Fathers. Mohammed was presumably influenced by their teaching.)

5. Each human being has two recording angels, who stand invisibly on each side of him or her. The angel on the left records one's sins. The angel on the right records one's good deeds. The good and bad deeds are totalled and balanced on the Day of Judgment. Permission to enter Paradise will be given only to those whose good deeds outweigh their bad ones. (These ideas, too, were probably influenced by similar early Christian speculations about the functions of angels.)

6. There are bad angels and good ones. Al Sharitan, the devil, is a fallen angel who was cast out of heaven for disobeying Allah. He is the ruler of evil spirits, and the tempter who leads people into sin.

The next chapter will begin a study of the Christian view of angels.

CHAPTER TWO

ANGELS AND THE CHURCH

> I throw myself down in my chamber, and I call in and invite God and his angels hither, and when they are there, I neglect God and his angels, for the noise of a fly, for the rattling of a coach, for the whining of a door. *(John Donne, from a sermon preached in 1626)*

How sadly easy it is for distraction to capture us! How soon we lose awareness of the spiritual dimension in which we actually live, a dimension more real than the material things that so readily engross us. Yet they will all vanish, and only the realm of God and the angels will remain. We should assiduously cultivate our spiritual perception, praying with Elisha, *"Lord, open our eyes, that we may see!"* (2 Kg 6:17). Then it may happen again as it did for the prophet's servant: *"The Lord opened the eyes of the young man, and he saw; and behold, the mountain was full of horses and chariots of fire round about Elisha!"*

That heavenly host still surrounds the servants of God. They are our allies. Scripture is plain in its witness that they constantly exercise a great influence upon human affairs. A sense of their presence, of their awesome strength, can be wonderfully encouraging!

Nonetheless, we do need to be content with that biblical witness alone, avoiding the kinds of empty speculations we looked at in the previous chapter. On that issue, Martin Luther had a wise word -

> Moses writes nothing about the creation of angels because, to begin with, he describes only the creation of matters visible. In the second place, he did not want to provide an opportunity for

speculation. Our God did the right thing in that he did not permit many matters to be written; otherwise we would have despised what we now have and would have pried into what is beyond us. [15]

What quarrels we would avoid, what grief remain unknown, if scholars were content not to "pry into what is beyond us"! But they have dared to search where there was no light, and will probably continue to dare, so it is no surprise if they find themselves trapped in confusion. Yet truly wise men have given enough warning. Long before Luther, that savvy old scribe Sirach gave this admonition to his young students -

Do not pry into things too hard for you
or examine what is beyond your reach.
Meditate on the commandments you have been given;
what the Lord keeps secret is no concern of yours.
Do not busy yourself with matters that are beyond you;
even what has been shown you is above man's grasp.
Many have been led astray by their speculations,
and false conjectures have impaired their judgment (Sir 3:21-24).

Curiosity, according to the fable, once killed an incautious cat. It can still be perilous to be inquisitive beyond what God has revealed. I hope in these pages not to serve you so ill. It is safer to remain within the covers of the Bible.

So you will find here none of the pestilences that have plagued the church across the centuries, nor any of the virulent poisons of our own time. There will be no strange doctrines based on angelic visitations; no esoteric angelic names; no angelic prophecies about the future; no attempt to turn the angels into Christian slaves, bound to do this or that at your instant beck.

---

[15] What Luther Says, compiled by E. W. Plass; Concordia Pub. House, St Louis, Missouri; 1959; vol. 1, Angels, pg. 23:62.

There is enough wonder and joy in what has already been given to us in scripture. We need search no further to find wealth beyond measure and truth sufficient to establish the most timid soul in firm trust.

I. THE APOSTLES AND THE ANGELS

The apostolic authors all carefully avoided the wild speculations of the rabbis and the Greek philosophers, and also of the later Christian scholars. The NT speaks about angels only with restraint. What should we learn from that? Surely to avoid the faults of magnifying angels too much, or of being too curious about the secrets of their existence. Above all, repel with horror the idea of placing angels between yourself and Christ.

However, it is still fair to say that the NT generally adopts and endorses the angelology of the contemporary Jewish world, and that the latter was in its turn a development of the ideas contained in the OT.

The Bible shows that the Hebrews believed in angels from the dawn of their history, and they recognised and were grateful for the ministry of these splendid servants of God. However, their ideas about angels remained fragmentary throughout the period of the OT; the prophets and teachers of early Israel apparently felt no need to develop a systematic doctrine of angels.

But a change occurred in the spiritual consciousness of the people in the aftermath of their captivity in Babylon. They became much more aware of the invisible realm of the spirit, more sensitive to such matters as the existence and work of angels. Hence, after their return from exile, during the period between the two testaments, the rabbis began to develop their thinking about angels. By the time of Christ the doctrine had come to full flower - although not all Jews were convinced. The Sadducees, for example, rejected any elaborate doctrine of angels (Ac 23:8). They argued that everything not clearly a part of the original teaching of Moses is suspect, and must be discarded.

II. JESUS AND THE ANGELS

Jesus often referred to angels, although always in association with other more important themes. He does not seem ever to have made a statement specifically about the angels themselves. However, when his sayings are gathered together they are seen to comprise almost a complete angelology. Jesus generally endorsed commonly held Jewish opinions about angels, except in two areas:

♦ the restraint underlying his references to angels shows his disinterest in the wilder speculations of his contemporaries.

♦ he took pains to countermand the prevailing notion that prayer could reach God only through the angels.

Angels held a subsidiary place in the thought of Jesus, and he taught the people to come directly to the Father in his name. He sought to break down the multitude of barriers the people had erected between themselves and God.

Jesus speaks about angels in the following places: Mt 13:39,41,49; 16:27; 18:10; 22:30; 24:31,36; 25:31,41; 26:53; Lu 12:8,9; 15:10; 16:22; 20:36; Jn 1:51. See also Mt 6:10 - *"Thy will be done on earth as it is in heaven;"* which pre-supposes there are beings in heaven who are busy doing the Father's will. Not only do they do God's will, they do it so perfectly that Christ enjoins us to pray for skill to follow the same model of full obedience.

You can be sure that these pages will follow the example set by Christ. I will try to avoid the two follies of the past: unprofitable conjecture; and placing the angels between you and God.

THE USEFULNESS OF THE DOCTRINE

Although Christ was careful to countermand the Jewish tendency to push God ever further away from man by erecting barricades of angels, it is evidently wrong to assume he discredited the idea of angels, or ignored their importance in Christian life. Although we can have direct fellowship with God without angelic mediation, that does not mean there is no room for their ministry.

For example, Jesus declared, *"I could ask the Father, and he would send me more than twelve legions of angels"* (Mt 26:53).

Who did he pray to - an angel, or God? Plainly, he directed his prayer to the Father. He would ask God, not the angels, for help. But he allowed that the Father might choose to help him by sending angels to fight for him.

Angels therefore have an important function in serving God and in ministering to man. What that function is will become more apparent as this study unfolds, but some general comments will be appropriate here -

A. DIVERSE OPINIONS

Various groups of Christians hold quite diverse opinions about the role of angels in Christian belief and practice -

1. The Active View

Some credit angels with a high and active place in Christian life. They set great value on the support angels provide, in prayer and worship, and in protection and guidance. They believe angels are constantly serving man in heaven at the throne of God, and serving God on earth by ministering to man. In their view, angels are continually influencing our behaviour and the events that occur around us day by day. They see both their actions and those of the angels always intertwined, and they think of angels and man in partnership, working together for God.

For example, in his comment on Ps 91:11, C. H. Spurgeon writes:

> The protection here promised is exceeding broad as to place, for it refers to all our ways, and what do we wish for more? How angels thus keep us we cannot tell. Whether they repel demons, counteract spiritual plots, or even ward off the subtler physical forces of disease, we do not know. Perhaps we shall one day stand amazed at the multiplied services which the unseen hands have rendered us. [16]

Martin Luther had a similar opinion:

> That angels are with us is very sure, and no one should ever have doubted it. It is certain ... that they are truly around us in this life, providing for and guiding our affairs, if we would only firmly believe it ... Therefore we should learn that our best and most loyal friends are invisible. They are the good angels, who by their faithfulness and benevolence and by their many services of friendship greatly excel our visible friends ... (If) you see that something has turned out well, you should say, "The man had a good angel; otherwise, the matter would have turned out worse." For instance, it should not be called luck but the special work of good angels when a man is saved from drowning or when a stone falls upon someone without inflicting any particular harm ... That the entire world is not a mass of flames, that all towns and villages are not lying in a heap of ruins, we owe to the working and doing of the good angels. [17]

[16]   Treasury of David, Vol 2; pg. 93. Zondervan Publishing House, Grand Rapids, Michigan; 1974 reprint.

[17]   Op. cit., pg. 23:63, 25:66, 68.

2. The Passive View

Because of what the Bible says, some feel obliged to accept the existence of angels, but their belief remains a matter of theory only. They have no experience of angels, and they do not seek any angelic encounter. They dislike the thought of any sort of intermediary (save Christ) standing between them and God. Even if angels do exist, these sceptics still prefer to rely upon the Holy Spirit. They argue that angelic functions have been thoroughly superseded by the ministry of the Spirit, who is now our Comforter, Teacher, Guide, and Protector. The angels (they concede) may resume their visible activity when Christ returns, but in the meantime there is little or no place for them in the life of the church.

3. The Cautious View

Some reject the idea of angels being continually involved in human affairs, but they allow there are seasons of angelic visitation, that is, times when angels are very active, even visibly, on earth. For example, A. H. Strong writes:

> (The angels) are not to be considered as the mediating agents of God's regular and common providence in the affairs of his church. He "maketh his angels winds" and a "flaming fire", not in his ordinary procedure, but in connection with special displays of his power for moral ends (De 33:2; Ac 7:53; Ga 3:19; He 2:2). Their intervention is apparently occasional and exceptional - not at their own option, but only as it is permitted or commanded by God. Hence we are not to conceive of angels as coming between us and God, nor are we, without special revelation of the fact, to attribute to them in any particular case the effects which the scriptures generally ascribe to divine providence ... Angelic appearances generally mark

God's entrance upon new epochs in the unfolding of his plans. Hence we read of angels at the completion of creation (Jb 38:7); at the giving of the law (Ga 3:19); at the birth of Christ (Lu 2:13); at the two temptations in the wilderness and in Gethsemane (Mt 4:11; Lu 22:43); at the resurrection (Mt 28:2); at the ascension (Ac 1:10); at the final judgment (Mt 25:31) ... [18]

4. The Negative View

Some reject the very concept of angels, claiming Christ himself did not really believe in them, but merely accommodated himself to the prevailing viewpoint. When Jesus spoke about 'angels' (they say) he actually meant God himself, or whatever agency God might use, whether material or immaterial, to do his will.

However, in contrast with that view, note how Jesus mentioned angels, not only in parables and stories, where symbolism might be expected, but in passages of plain teaching. In those latter places, if he did not truly believe in the existence of angels, mention of them was not only unnecessary, but quite misleading. If he did not accept the prevailing notions about angels, yet was unwilling to denounce them, he could at least have avoided all reference to them.

Furthermore, Christ not only made frequent mention of angels, he linked them with the most basic aspects of the gospel; such as redemption, the resurrection, the second advent, the judgment, and so on (see references above).

The conclusion seems inescapable: Jesus truly believed in angels, and so should we; and we should also gain from this belief the same comfort and support he evidently did (cp. Mt 4:11; 26:53; Lu 22:43; Jn 1:51).

---

[18]   Op. cit., pg. 452-453.

B. SUPPORTING EVIDENCE

Beyond the biblical data, commentators have supported the doctrine of angels by various other arguments -

1. Since the gap between man and the lowest forms of life is filled with numberless gradations, it is possible that between man and God also there are creatures of higher than human intelligence.

2. It has been the disposition of man everywhere, from ancient times to modern, to believe in beings superior to himself yet inferior to the supreme deity. This universal belief is a presumptive argument in favour of these superior beings.

3. St Thomas Aquinas argued that angels possessed neither matter nor form, and that each one of the myriad angels is therefore a distinctly created individual intelligence -

> (The) angels are not of the same species ... For things which agree in species but differ in number, agree in form but are distinguished materially. If, therefore, the angels are not composed of matter and form, as was said above, it follows that it is impossible for two angels to be of one species; just as it would be impossible to say that there are several separate whitenesses, or several humanities, since whitenesses are not several, except insofar as they are in several substances ... Hence the perfection of the angelic nature requires the multiplying of species, but not the multiplying of individuals in one species.[19]

---

[19] *Summa Theologicae*, I.4.50.4. My quote taken from Basic Writings of Saint Thomas Aquinas, Vol. One; ed. Anton C. Pegis; Random House, New York; 1945; in. loc.

Which is to say, unlike the feline species (cats), or the canine species (dogs), or the human species, which have many individual members, each single angel is itself a complete species, with only one possible member. John Donne (1572-1631) reflected that idea in what was probably his last poem, an elegy upon the death of the young marquise Hamilton -

> Whether that soul which now comes up to you
> Fill any former rank or make a new,
> Whether it take a name named there before,
> Or be a name itself, and order more
> Than was in heaven till now (for may not he
> Be so, if every several angel be
> A kind alone?) what ever order grow
> Greater by him in heaven, we do not so;
> One of your orders grows by his access;
> But, by his loss grow all our orders less ...[20]

The idea of each angel constituting a distinct species was developed by F. L. Godet into an argument for the existence of angels. He stated that there are three forms of existence known to us

♦ the vegetable world: which we may call species without individuality;

♦ the animal world: which we may call individuality under bondage to the species;

♦ mankind: which we may call species overpowered by individuality;

---

[20] *An Hymn To The Saints, and to Marquise Hamilton*, lines 1-10. The marquise was only 36 when he died, "at the height of a glittering career in the Scots and English courts." John Donne, <u>The Complete English Poems</u>, ed. A. J. Smith; Penguin Books; 1982; pg. 264,592.

◆ which makes at least one other form of existence possible: individuality without species; that is, lacking parents, with each member being individually created. That could describe the angels.[21]

Whether such arguments make enough sense, or have enough importance, to deserve your attention, you will have to determine for yourself. It perhaps violates my own canon of not going beyond scripture. Still, I do find it interesting, though not compelling.

III. GUARD AGAINST A CULT OF ANGELS

A. NO ANGEL SHOULD BE WORSHIPPED

Whatever place angels may have in the economy of God, and whatever aid they may render us, scripture is adamant that prayer should not be addressed to them.

Give the angels honour. But never worship. Paul stringently commanded the Colossians to stop venerating mere messengers of God -

> *Let no one disqualify you (as Christians), insisting on self-abasement and worship of angels, taking his stand on visions, puffed up without reason by his sensuous mind (2:18).*

Notice how Paul associates the false piety of self-abasement with the worship of angels. Those two corrupt spiritual expressions are often found together.

When John saw an angel he *"fell down at his feet to worship him"*; but the angel urgently commanded him, *"You must not do that! I am a fellow servant with you and your brethren who hold the testimony of Jesus. Worship God!"* (Re 19:10). A little later, under the awesome impact of another angelic visitation, John could not help himself, and once more he *"fell down to worship at the feet of*

---

[21]   I have lost the source of this summary of Godet's argument.

the angel". But again, and with the same urgency, the angel repeated, *"You must not do that! I am a fellow servant with you and your brethren the prophets, and with those who keep the words of this book. Worship God!"* (22:9; see also 15:3-4; De 6:13-15).

The repetition of those two scenes in the Apocalypse, plus various references in the Fathers, show that a cult of angels had developed very early in the church, and remained a threat for many years. Strenuous, and at least partially successful, efforts were made to stamp it out.

In our thinking, believing, and practice, we must find a place for angels that comes well short of addressing any kind of prayer to them, or of according them any kind of worshipful veneration. Never do more than respect them as holy and perfect servants of God.

In his saying about the *"twelve legions"*, Jesus did suggest you can gain the ministry of angels by prayer (Mt 26:53). Nonetheless, it is probably improper to ask specifically for angelic assistance. Almost certainly it is better simply to request divine help, and leave it to the discretion of God whether he chooses to work through angels.

For example, when Peter was in prison the church earnestly prayed to God for him, and the Lord saw fit to rescue him by an angel (Ac 12:5,7); but it is unlikely the church asked for angelic intervention. They probably had no idea how God would answer their prayer. Even after Peter was safely with his friends, they attributed the apostle's rescue, not to the angel, but to the Lord (vs. 11,17).

B. NO ANGEL SHOULD BE ADDRESSED IN PRAYER

Contrary to the 16th century Council of Trent, which taught that angels intercede for men and that "it is good and profitable to invoke them suppliantly ... for the purpose of obtaining benefits from God through his Son Jesus Christ,"[22] we insist that prayer must not be directed to an angel, but to God alone.

> *For there is one God, and there is one mediator between God and men, the man Christ Jesus, who gave himself as a ransom for all (1 Ti 2:5-6).*

> *Truly, truly, I say to you, if you ask anything of the Father, he will give it to you in my name. Hitherto you have asked nothing in my name; ask, and you will receive, that your joy may be full (Jn 16:23-24).*

Notice also Mt 26:53, how Jesus did not pray to the angels, but to the Father -

> *Do you think that I cannot appeal to my Father, and he will at once send me more than twelve legions of angels?*

The passage is remarkable also for its deliberate reversal of the popular Jewish idea that the best way to reach God was through various heavenly intermediaries. On the contrary, Jesus implied, the angels had to be reached through God!

C. NO REVELATION BEYOND SCRIPTURE

1. Paul gives a most emphatic warning against receiving any teaching from an angel that differs from what has already been revealed in scripture -

> *Even if we, or an angel from heaven, should preach to you a gospel contrary to that which you received, let him be accursed. As we have said before, so now I say again, If any one is preaching to you a gospel contrary to that which you received, let him be accursed (Ga 1:8,9; and cp. also Ju 3).*

---

[22]   Quoted from <u>The New International Dictionary of the Christian Church</u>; ed. J. D. Douglas; Paternoster Press, Exeter, UK.; 1974; article, Angels.

The problem of people being led astray by angelic revelations has long plagued the church, and still does. As far back as the 3rd century a Roman presbyter, Gaius, furiously denounced a certain Cerinthus, who was preaching corrupt doctrine based on things he claimed an angel had shown him -

> But Cerinthus, by means of revelations which he pretended were written by a great apostle, also false pretended to wonderful things, as if they were showed him by angels, asserting that after the resurrection there would be an earthly kingdom of Christ, and that the flesh ... would be subject to desires and pleasures. Being also an enemy of the divine scriptures, with a view to deceive men, he said that there would be a space of a thousand years for celebrating nuptial festivals[23].

Apparently Cerinthus was promulgating a carnal and sensuous interpretation of the Apocalypse, saying that the millennial kingdom "would consist in those things that he craved in the gratification of appetite and lust; that is, in eating, drinking, marrying ... " To authenticate his views he claimed special revelation given to him by an angel.

Cerinthus, at least for the early part of his life, was a contemporary of the apostle John, and Eusebius records this quaint anecdote about him -

> Irenaeus ... gives some more abominable false doctrines of the same man ... (and) relates a story which deserves to be recorded. He says, on the authority of Polycarp, that the apostle John once entered a bath to bathe; but, learning that Cerinthus

---

[23]   The quote is taken from Eusebius' early 4th century <u>Church History</u>, Bk 3, ch. 28; tr. C. F. Cruse; Baker Book House; a 1977 reprint of a mid-19th century translation. The next few lines in your chapter come from the same place.

was within, he sprang from the place and rushed out of the door, for he could not bear to remain under the same roof with him. And he advised those that were with him to do the same, saying, "Let us flee, lest the bath fall; for Cerinthus, the enemy of truth, is within!"[24]

Would God that Christian leaders today would have the same horror of doctrinal contamination!

But in any case, hear nothing from any supernatural visitor unless it conforms closely to scripture.

2. You may feel that no lying spirit could ever deceive you. But beware! Even fallen angels can have a beautiful appearance, and may also seem to work miracles; see 2 Co 11:13-14; 1 Th 5:21; 1 Jn 4:1; 1 Ti 4:1. Always the criterion must be -

> *When they say to you, "Seek those who are mediums and wizards, who whisper and mutter," should not a people seek their God? Should they seek the dead on behalf of the living? To the law and to the testimony! If they do not speak according to this word, it is because there is no light in them (Is 8:19-20, NKJ).*

3. It seems that angels can be sent by God to give an insight into the future (cp. Re 17:1; etc); and they can also bring some instruction or command (cp. Ac 5:17-21). Yet still I caution you to test each instance. You will not offend God if you are simply taking scrupulous care not to be misled. He will be angry only if, having given you sufficient proof of dealing with a genuine angel, you refuse to obey the divine will.

---

[24] The Nicene and Post-Nicene Fathers, Second Series, Volume One, *Eusebius*; Eerdman's Pub. Co, Grand Rapids, Michigan; 1979 reprint of the 1890 edition. The passage comes from the same place in the *Church History* as the one cited in the previous footnote.

One good test is this: any "angel" who obscures the vision of God, who takes attention away from Christ, who draws your eye to its own beauty, who arouses more excitement in you or seems more appealing than Christ, does not come from the Father's presence. Whoever is a true servant of God will glorify God and cause you to pronounce that Jesus is Lord (1 Co 12:1-3).

D. NOTHING BETWEEN YOU AND GOD

As I have already mentioned, some of the early Christians were prone to place between themselves and God a vast series of angels, each ranked a little higher than the other; nor did they hesitate to pray to those angels and to seek their mediation in heaven.

For example, Irenaeus (c. 190) sternly opposed the teaching of Basilides, an Alexandrine thinker of the early 2nd century. In his work Against Heresies I.24.3-7, Irenaeus writes -

> Basilides ... gives an immense development to his doctrines. He sets forth that Mind was first born of the unborn Father, that from him, again, was born Logos, from Logos Prudence, from Prudence Wisdom and Power, and from Power and Wisdom the powers, and princes, and angels, whom he also calls the first; and that by them the first heaven was made. Then other powers, being formed by emanation from these, created another heaven similar to the first; and in like manner, when, others again, had been formed by emanation from them, corresponding exactly to those above them, these two framed another third heaven; and then from this third, in downward order, there was a fourth succession of descendants; and so on, after the same fashion, they declare that more princes and angels were formed ... Those angels who occupy the lowest heaven, that, namely, which is visible to us, formed all things which are in the world, and made

allotments among themselves of the earth and of those nations which are upon it.

According to Basilides, there were at least 365 heavens ranked one above the other, conforming to the number of days in an earth year! How distant the actual throne of God must have seemed!

Paul sternly rebuked such absurd notions; Cl 1:15-19; 2:4,8- 10; etc. Never doubt it. You have perfect, instant, and free access to the most intimate presence of God, simply by the blood of Jesus (He 10:19-23). Allow no angel, no matter how grand, to stand between you and the Father's breast.

IV. ANGELS ARE LIMITED AND DEPENDENT

Unlike God, angels cannot create an object out of nothing; they cannot do a miracle of their own volition nor by their own unaided power; they cannot act without the means to do so; they cannot uninvited search into the human mind.

Although their strength and wisdom are greater than ours, they are still, like us, dependent beings; they can do nothing, nor hold anything, save what God allows.

It would seem that angels can "influence men only in ways analogous to those by which men influence each other" (Strong); except that their superior strength, mobility, access to heaven's resources, and so on, may give a supernatural character to their activities.

Therefore, while it is no doubt proper to recognise the existence and functions of angels, we ought not to think of them so much as of their captain, Jesus Christ, our Lord and theirs. The victories they gain are his, and the honour is his, for without him their purpose would fail.

Illustration: in the history of Israel, it is said that "David" destroyed the Philistines, or conquered Moab, and so on, when the battle was actually fought by soldiers under his command. Yet without him there would have been no army, nor any triumph. Likewise, Christ may choose to send out his angels and to accomplish his purpose by their agency; but the glory belongs not to the servants, but to him, the Master. The scriptures are emphatic in asserting that all angels are subject to Christ:

- ◆ (God has made Christ) sit at his right hand in the heavenly places, far above all rule and power and authority and dominion, and above every name that is named, not only in this age but also in that which is to come (Ep 1:20-21).

- ◆ For in Christ all things were created, in heaven and on earth, visible and invisible, whether thrones or dominions or principalities or authorities (Cl 1:16).

- ◆ Christ is the head of all rule and authority (2:10).

- ◆ Christ has gone into heaven and is at the right hand of God, with angels, authorities, and powers subject to him (1 Pe 3:22).

V. ANGELS AND OUR SALVATION

A. ANGELS ARE AFFECTED BY THE CROSS

The angels are deeply involved in our salvation, and vitally interested in the welfare of the church, for apparently the cross of Christ touches their existence as it does ours.

Scripture suggests that the cross unites the angelic creation with redeemed humanity. Hence their interaction with the church is not merely a matter of obedience to divine command, but also a thing of deep personal involvement. Their destiny and ours are inextricably linked. The success of the church is their gain; the failure of the church is their loss. That is why Jesus affirmed,

> *There will be more joy in heaven over one sinner*
> *who repents than over ninety-nine righteous persons*
> *who need no repentance ... Just so, I tell you, there*

is joy before the angels of God over one sinner who
repents (Lu 15:7,10).

Paul spoke about the mystery of God's eternal plan; but he was
sure that the fulfilment of that plan, for the entire creation,
including the angels, cannot be separated from the church -

> *I preach ... to make all men see what is the plan of*
> *the mystery hidden for ages in God who created all*
> *things; that through the church the manifold*
> *wisdom of God might now be made known to the*
> *principalities and powers in the heavenly places (Ep*
> *3:9,10).*

The angels know and delight in the gospel. They were witnesses of
the birth, death, and resurrection of Jesus. They search out the
mystery of salvation as earnestly as any saint, and with the same
expectation of future glory (1 Ti 3:16; 1 Pe 1:12). Angels were
present, and actively involved, at every stage of the drama of
redemption:

- they announced the conception of John (Lu 1:13,36)

- they shared in the birth of Christ (Mt 1:20,21; Lu 1:31;
  2:10-12)

- they were present in the wilderness (Mt 4:11)

- they witnessed the agony in the garden (Lu 22:43)

- they were present at the resurrection (Mt 28:5-7; Lu 24:23)

- they announced Jesus' ascension and return (Ac 1:11).

We should think of the angels then as in some way fellow-heirs
with us of the coming glory. The fall of man did not leave them
unhurt. They are part of *"the creation (that) waits with eager*
longing for the revealing of the sons of God"; they are part of *"the*
creation (that) has been groaning in travail together until now".
They too are looking forward to *"obtaining the glorious liberty of*

the children of God" when Christ returns and raptures his church. For these reasons it is their deep joy to serve the church and to minister to the children of God. (See Ro 8:18-23).

B. IN PARTNERSHIP WITH THE CHURCH

From what I have said so far it seems we should think of the angels as our partners in the service of God. They are not part of the church, but they, like we, are workers in the kingdom of our Father. They labour together with us, and they also minister to us. In some way their future happiness and ours are linked; the fulfilment of their destiny will flow out of our redemption.

However, it is difficult to determine how intimately or how often angels affect your daily affairs or mine. Persons of a mystic disposition will probably see angelic intervention in even the most insignificant events; whereas more pragmatic minds may rarely, if ever, recognise angelic influence. The truth possibly sits somewhere in the middle.

It seems fair to assume that angels intervene in our lives more often, and more effectively, than most of us imagine; but it is unlikely they are perpetually hovering over each saint, influencing every action, every word, every event. More plausibly - like those particular occasions when angels came to minister to Christ, or to release Peter from prison, and so on - they touch your life, and mine, only when they are specifically dispatched by God to render us assistance.

Nonetheless, there is at least a popular belief that angels do concern themselves with human affairs, and that their own happiness is affected for good or ill by the human condition (cp. Mt 18:10; Lu 4:10; 15:7,10; etc). The influential English poet and journalist Leigh Hunt (1784-1859) captured something of this idea of angelic interest in human life in his best-known poem, *Abou Ben Adhem* -

Abou Ben Adhem (may his tribe increase)

Awoke one night from a deep dream of peace,
And saw, within the moonlight in his room,
Making it rich, and like a lily in bloom-
An angel, writing in a book of gold.
Exceeding peace had made Ben Adhem bold,
And to the presence in the room he said,
    "What writest thou?"- The vision raised its head,
And, with a look made of all sweet accord,
Answered, "The names of those who love the Lord."
    "And is mine one?" said Abou. "Nay, not so,"
Replied the angel. Abou spoke more low,
But cheerly still, and said, "I pray thee, then,
Write me as one that loves his fellow men."
The angel wrote, and vanish'd. The next night
It came again with a great wakening light,
And show'd the names whom love of God had blessed,
And lo! Ben Adhem's name led all the rest.

In a very different tone, the angels may also be agents of divine vengeance upon an ungodly people. This is an idea that I will explore in more detail later. In the meantime, Lord Byron's poem about the destruction of Sennacherib's army (2 Kg 19:35-36) conveys a vivid picture of angelic fury -

The Assyrian came down like a wolf on the fold,
And his cohorts were gleaming in purple and gold;
And the sheen on their spears was like stars on the sea,
When the blue wave rolls nightly on deep Galilee.

Like the leaves of the forest when Summer is green,
That host with their banners at sunset were seen:

Like the leaves of the forest when autumn hath
blown,
That host on the morrow lay withered and strown.

For the Angel of Death spread his wings on the
blast,
And breathed in the face of the foe as he passed;
And the eyes of the sleepers waxed deadly and chill,
And their hearts but once heaved, and for ever grew
still!

And the widows of Ashur are loud in their wail,
And the idols are broke in the temple of Baal;
And the might of the Gentile, unsmote by the
sword,
Hath melted like snow in the glance of the Lord!

- st. 1,2,3,6.

CHAPTER THREE

WHAT ARE ANGELS LIKE?

Somewhere around the year 200 one of the great teachers of the early church, Origen, wrote -

> This also is a part of the teaching of the Church, that there are certain angels of God ... which are his servants in accomplishing the salvation of men. When these, however, were created or of what nature they are, or how they exist, is not clearly stated (in scripture).[25]

Unhappily, there has not been much progress since then! We still have no clear knowledge about the origin of the angels (except that God created them); nor is there any certainty about their true nature. But we are not left wholly ignorant. Some things can be defined from scripture -

I. THEIR APPEARANCE

A. ROMANTICISED

For several centuries the church sought to humanise the angels, to make them less objects of awe and more objects of playful or sentimental devotion. In the Middle Ages the mighty cherubim who surrounded Yahweh's throne with glory, were turned into chubby cherubs, obviously human, not at all awesome, merely a Christianised version of the Greek god Cupid.

Female angels became popular in Italy early in the Renaissance. They were painted in various states of undress and in changing conformity to the prevailing fashions. They became creatures of

---

[25] *Principles*, Pref. 10. From The Ante-Nicene Fathers, Vol. 4; Eerdman's Pub. Co., Grand Rapids, Michigan; 1979 reprint of the 1885 edition; pg. 241.

beauty, but emptied of strength and majesty; easy to admire, but hardly a being before which a man would fall prostrate, as Daniel and John did when they saw the angel of God.

Martin Luther was unimpressed by that image -

> The good angels bring terror, that is, they come with a certain majesty ... so that people to whom they come are frightened. Thus Mary is filled with fear upon seeing the angel (Lu 1:29) ... But an evil angel creeps along smoothly and gently, like a serpent, until he has lured men into security and sin; then he departs, leaving horrible fear behind.[26]

B. FEMINISED

1. Like A Woman With Wings

Snowy garments, magnificent wings, feminine (or at least asexual) appearance - that became the stereotyped image of an angel, and it is still widely popular. Nor is it without some scriptural foundation-

> *Then I lifted my eyes and saw, and behold, two women coming forward! The wind was in their wings; they had wings like the wings of a stork ... !*
> *(Zc 5:9)*

However, that, as far as I can discover, is the only place in scripture where an angel looked like a woman. More commonly (as I will discuss in more detail below), when angels became visible they took on the shape of an adult man.

But what about those wings?

The popular image of winged angels is not endorsed by scripture. On the few occasions angels did appear with wings the sight was

---

[26]   Op. cit., 26:29.

so extraordinary the biblical writers drew special attention to it (Is 6:2; Zc 5:9).

So once again, when angels made themselves visible, they usually did so in a male form, and they conformed to contemporary language, dress, and social customs. They could hardly have done otherwise in that ancient and very patriarchal culture. Their very mission would have been jeopardised if they had come in the shape of a woman.

In Section (III)(C)(3)(a) below, you will find a more detailed description of the human appearance of many angelic visitors.

2. Androgynous Angels

The Second Council of Nicaea (787) decided that it was lawful to represent angels in pictures, and this led to stylisation of the members of the nine choirs, based on scriptural descriptions given in the visions of the prophets Isaiah (6;1- 2) and Ezekiel (1:4-14), and deduction from other biblical texts ... Angels were also thought to be supremely beautiful and were therefore portrayed as handsome boys and comely women, but as they were considered to be sexless, they were given an androgynous appearance. For modesty's sake they were clothed in a ... flowing garment which covered their feet.[27]

So it remains in art to this day. But how reliable that image is, you will have to decide for yourself. Perhaps the following anecdote will keep you cautious. It is about the famous 16th century artist known to us as El Greco -

There is ... a story that he was once "interviewed" by the Inquisition because according to its learned theologians his paintings were heretical. The indictment was that the wings of the

---

[27]   Dictionary Of Christian Lore, pg. 26.

angels he painted were larger than was considered "natural", therefore "he was correcting the Lord's creation" - and was a heretic!

> "Certainly, since you accuse me, you must have seen angels yourselves," remarked Greco.

> "No, we have not."

> "Then the learned theologians must have seen them."

> "No, they haven't either. Why the question?"

> "Because if you had, I would beg you to take me there so that I could copy exactly the length and the texture of their wings. However, since neither you, nor the theologians, nor I have ever seen angels, how come my paintings are considered heretic?"

> "Because we have never seen in a religious painting, angels with such large wings."

> "Yet, since you declare that you have never seen angels, how can you prove to me that the length of the angel's wings in all other pictures is not as arbitrary as mine?"

The Inquisitors, not being able to find an answer - so the story goes - pronounced him innocent![28]

II. THEIR ANTIQUITY

A. CREATED BEFORE THE EARTH

The Bible contains references to angels from Genesis to Revelation; they were seen in many lands, and they were active at all stages of the history of Israel. Outside of the Bible, the earliest

---

[28] International History Magazine, Editions Horizons, Lausanne, Switzerland; Sept. 1973; pg. 97.

archaeological evidence of angels to date appears on the stele of Ur-Nammus (c. 2250 BC), which depicts angels as flying over the head of the king while he was in prayer. The Assyrians and Babylonians venerated beings akin to angels - half human, half animal, with large wings; but those pagan winged-creatures were more like demon gods than like biblical angels.

The Bible says that the angels are glorious and majestic beings whom God created long before he made man. The psalmist, for example, calls upon all the elements of creation to praise God in the order in which he made them, and he places the angels at the top of his list, ahead even of the sun, moon, and stars, and well ahead of man -

> *Praise the Lord from the heavens, praise him in the heights! Praise him, all his angels; praise him, all his host! Praise him sun and moon; praise him, all you shining stars ... For he commanded, and they were created (Ps 148:2-5).*

The Lord reminded Job that the angels (whom he called *"the sons of God"*) were present, and shouting with joy, when the foundations of the earth were laid (Job 38:4-7); hence the angels were created before God called the earth into being. For this reason, since they were made before man, they stand higher than man in the order of things - but not for ever, for God has appointed a day when redeemed man will be given a higher status than angels-

> *What is man that you are mindful of him, or the son of man, that you care for him? "you made him for a little while lower than the angels ... (He 2:5-7)*

The apostle adds (vs. 5, 8) that *"the world to come"* will not come under the rule of angels, for God has given that right to redeemed man. Indeed, everything in the new creation, including the angels, will be subject to the authority of the glorified church. Paul is even more emphatic -

Do you not know that the saints will judge the world?...Do you not know that we are to judge angels? (1 Co 6:2-3).

B. CREATED BY CHRIST

Remember always that angels are not some species of lesser deity. They are created beings, just as we are. They were created *"in Christ, through Christ, and for Christ"*. Paul included them in the great affirmation he made to the Corinthians -

> *There is one God, the Father, from whom are all things ... and one Lord, Jesus Christ, through whom are all things (Cl 1:16; 1 Co 8:6; and cp. Ex 20:11).*

See also He 1:7, *"He makes his angels winds, and his servants flames of fire"*; which is taken from the LXX version of Ps 104:4. Paul uses that passage to show that the angels, in contrast with Christ, are mutable and transitory things (like wind and fire).

A similar idea occurs in 2 Esdras 8:21 -

> *O Lord, who dost inhabit eternity, to whom the sky and the highest heavens belong; whose throne is beyond imagining, and whose glory is past conceiving; who art attended by the host of angels, trembling as they turn themselves into wind and fire at thy bidding ... (NEB; part of a supposed prayer by the biblical scribe Ezra).*

Never allow any angelic visitor to entice out of you anything that resembles worship.

III. THEIR ASSOCIATION

A. ANGELS AND HUMANITY

1. SERVANTS WITH US

Since God created every angel, they must be seen as no more than *"fellow-servants"* with us of the same Father. For a person to offer them worship is utterly abhorrent to them (Re 19:10; 22:9). Mark at once, not as God's holy servant, but as one of those evil angels who *"did not keep their own position but left their proper dwelling,"* any angelic visitor who invites worship. All such are already under the severe judgment of God (Ju 6). None but servants of Satan accept worship that belongs to God alone (Cl 2:18; Re 9:20; Mt 4:8- 10).

Popular opinion often reckons angels are glorified human spirits, supposing that death changes righteous men and women into angels. That is absurd. Angels are creatures distinct from man, preceding man in order of creation, and for the time being occupying a higher status than man in the government of God. They are plainly stronger than we are, and they appear in some respects to have a higher level of intelligence. But they have not been, nor will they ever be human. Neither will we ever be angels.

2. STATUS ABOVE US

However, to say we are now below the angels in status does not mean the angels represent a superior form of being, nor that we should think of ourselves as inferior to angels. Superior strength, even superior wisdom, does not always mean superiority of nature or being. Many animals, for example, are much stronger than man; one person may also have wisdom far above another; but that neither places the animals higher than man, nor makes one man inferior to another.

Hence, the apostle describes us as *"the first-born"*, and he shows the angels waiting in heaven for the saints to take their rightful place -

> *You have come to Mount Zion and to the city of the living God, the heavenly Jerusalem, and to innumerable angels in festal gathering, and to the assembly of the first-born who are enrolled in heaven (He 12:22-23).*

Jesus said that in the resurrection we shall be *"as the angels"* (Mt 22:30). He may have intended to imply only that sexual distinctions will vanish in the resurrection, without saying anything about the respective status of angels and men. But it seems better to infer that the resurrection will elevate man alongside the angels, and reveal that we are equal, if not superior, to them in our being. At least we are forbidden to have a reverential awe of angels. Respect and admiration, yes; but a sense of ignoble inferiority, no.

B. INDIVIDUALLY MADE

Another distinction between angels and man lies in their origin and propagation. We are a race; the angels are a company. They are created; we are begotten. In this we are much nearer to Christ than they are. He, like us, was *"begotten"* not created, and the apostle makes this the strongest mark of his superiority to the angels -

> *For to what angel did God ever say, "Thou art my Son, today I have begotten thee?"... And again, when he brings the first- born into the world, he says, "Let all the angels of God worship him" (He. 1:5-6).*

If being *"begotten"* rather than separately created suggests a higher form of being, then we must share with Christ his superiority to angels. In fact, we have a double claim to higher status: we are born (not made) both naturally and supernaturally, of human parentage and of divine, of the flesh and of the Spirit!

Unlike man, the angels do not spring from a common progenitor; the mystical links of relationship that join the human family do not bind them. The life they have springs from individual rivulets; they do not share a single stream, they were not born from a single seed. Scripture calls us sons of men, but you will search in vain for a son of an angel. They were separately created, and presumably their number is fixed.[29] They cannot at their own discretion infinitely multiply themselves as we can. Their number is immense, but still limited, and apparently the Lord God is not increasing that number by additional creation.

The assumption in scripture seems to be that their entire company was created in a moment by divine fiat, and this work is now complete for ever.

What about the fallen angels? We fell collectively into sin through our common progenitors (Adam and Eve). But it seems that each apostate angel fell separately and by deliberate choice. Perhaps that is the reason why scripture asserts Christ offers no redemption to the fallen angels, but only to the race of Adam -

For surely it is not with angels that he is concerned but with the descendants of (Adam) *(He 2:16; see also vs. 14-18).*

A. ATTRIBUTES OF ANGELS

1. GENERAL CONSENSUS

Among Christians who take the biblical data on angels seriously there is a general consensus that angels -

♦   are spiritual beings; normally invisible and intangible

---

[29]   See again the comment by St Thomas Aquinas on page 6 of chapter 2, para. (3).

- are incorporeal; not having fixed substance or form

- are non-human; distinct from man in origin, nature, mode of existence, and destiny

- were created before man; but are not superior to man

- are rational; having a power of thought and of communication

- are industrious; active and powerful in doing God's will

- are moral; capable of choice for good or evil

- are immortal; not being naturally subject to death

- exist in different hierarchies; but the number of ranks, and their nature, is unknown

- exercise a guardianship over mankind; but not necessarily over each individual person

- are worshipful; diligent in praise and adoration of God.

However, within that broad spectrum there are many differences of opinion, and not all commentators would accept every point of even the above outline. So I cannot claim exactitude for what follows, although it will represent what I think are the ideas accepted by most conservative scholars.

2. ANGELS ARE SPIRITS

He makes his angels winds, and his servants flames of fire ... Are they not all ministering spirits sent forth to serve, for the sake of those who are to obtain salvation *(He 1:7, 14)*.

a. Visible and Invisible

Although angels are able to assume a visible form, in their ordinary state they are insubstantial, incorporeal, intangible. That is, they do not have and do not require bodies. They can, and normally do exist without need to inhabit a physical frame or to take a material form. Thus they differ from man, in whom spiritual and physical are fixed in one being.

God has indeed made man to be primarily a spiritual being; but the human spirit is so designed that it can find full expression only through a body. Man cannot truly exist as a pure spirit. Without a body his soul is *"naked"* and it craves a *"house"* in which to live. Thus he cannot be content, after death, merely to be with Christ as a spirit. He longs and waits eagerly for the day of resurrection, which will clothe him with a glorious new *"spiritual body"* (1 Co 15:44; 2 Co 5:1- 4).

But in variance from man, while angels may assume a material and visible form, they have no necessity to do so in order to be true to their own nature. If they do enter the physical world in human form, it is solely for man's benefit, not because their capabilities depend on it.

At present our mortal frame restricts our access to the spiritual dimension; even in our own world we suffer many cramping limitations. The resurrection will loose us from these shackles (as Jesus was loosed, Lu 24:36-39; etc.), and the glorified children of God will be able to move freely from natural to spiritual, and have perfect control in both spheres. In the meantime, among all the creatures of God, only the angels have free intercourse with both heaven and earth, suffering no limitations except those imposed by their own natures, and by their obedience to the will of God - see Ge 28:12; Ac 12:7.

b. Angelic Motion

Angels move, but their method of locomotion differs from ours. They do not expend physical energy, nor are they confined to moving in one plane, as we are. When Ezekiel saw a vision of angels, they appeared to be like men with wings, and they also appeared to be moving in four directions at the same time - 1:5-6,9,12,17; 10:9-14.

The psalmist sang -

> *With mighty chariotry, twice ten thousand, thousands upon thousands, the Lord came from Sinai into the holy place (Ps 68:17).*

The angels are numbered in that verse; which means they can be counted. Therefore, they are distinct entities, separate from each other, and occupying a specific zone. They are spirits possessing definition, although we cannot grasp the contours of that definition.

c. Angelic Boundaries

Except for God, we find it difficult to imagine anything existing as a pure spirit, because we cannot conceive how the boundaries of a spirit can be defined. We do not have this problem in imagining God, for we accept that he has no boundaries, he is omnipresent. But created spirits, such as angels, must have some confining limits; there must be some restraint to their mode of existence. The old argument about how many angels could stand on the point of a pin was an attempt to explain the relationship of angels to space. Do they occupy a measurable space, or is that irrelevant for a pure spirit?

It is perhaps easier to say what angels are not than to say what they are. They are not omnipotent nor omnipresent. Restraints are imposed upon their power and movement. There are many things they cannot do. One of those is to be in two places at once, or to move instantaneously from one place to another. The scriptures portray angels not only moving from point to point, but also requiring time to make their journeys. They may be spirits, but they are nonetheless specific entities, existing within a definite framework. They are not limitless. They are bounded by a restraining law of God that determines the confines of their being.

That concept is easy to accept, but impossible to visualise. For us, all boundaries are physical; we cannot imagine how a frame can exist for an invisible and ethereal spirit. Our minds fragment when we try to define the limits of an unseen being. So we must be content to accept that angels are pure spirits, yet picture them in human form.[30]

3. THEY APPEAR IN VARIOUS FORMS

Although angels are usually invisible, countless men and women from ancient times until today claim to have seen them, and they have left a record of those preternatural encounters. Animals also have seen angels, sometimes when human eyes were blinded to the heavenly visitor - see Nu 22:21-35.

Excepting the cherubim and seraphim (which are discussed below), angels consistently appeared in human form, sometimes with a supernatural aspect, at other times so natural they were mistaken for ordinary men. Angels once appeared in feminine form (Zc 5:9), but (contrary to the impression left by some artists, and to heathen mythology) never as children, nor as animals.

---

[30]   Contrary to the opinion expressed above, A. A. Hodge writes: "Angels are called in the scriptures 'spirits' (*pneuma*), He 1:14, a word which is also used to designate the souls of men when separate from the body - 1 Pe 3:19. There is however nothing in that word, nor in the opinions of the Jews at the time of Christ, nor in anything which is told us of the nature or the employment of the angels in the scriptures, which prove that angels are absolutely destitute of proper material bodies of any kind. Indeed, as the Son of God is to have a 'glorious body', a 'spiritual body' forever, and since all the redeemed are to have bodies like his, and since the angels are associated with redeemed men as members of the same infinitely exalted kingdom, it may appear probable that angels may have been created with physical organisation not altogether dissimilar to the 'spiritual' bodies of the redeemed. They always appeared and spoke to men in Bible times in the bodily form of men, and as such they ate food and lodged in houses like common men - Ge 18:8, 19:3." From: Outlines of Theology; Eerdman's Publishing Company, Grand Rapids, Michigan, 1949; pg. 252.

a. They Appear in Human Form

i. With a supernatural shape

Although angels often appear in human form, sometimes their appearance has such a supernatural aspect that awe, astonishment, even fear, overwhelms those who see them (Lu 1:12; 24:4-5; etc.).

See also 1 Ch 21:16. Although there are earlier references to angels holding swords, this appears to be the first time scripture describes an angel with giant stature, hovering between heaven and earth -

> *David looked up and saw the angel of the Lord standing between heaven and earth, with a drawn sword in his hand extended over Jerusalem. Then David and the elders clothed themselves in sackcloth and fell upon their faces.*

Daniel had a similar encounter with a majestic angel, and he has left us a graphic description -

> *On the twenty-fourth day of the first month, as I was standing on the bank of the great river, that is, the Tigris, I lifted up my eyes and looked, and behold, a man clothed in linen, whose loins were girded with gold of Uphaz. His body was like beryl, his face like the appearance of lightning, his eyes like flaming torches, his arms and legs like the gleam of burnished bronze, and the sound of his words like the noise of a multitude. And I, Daniel, alone saw the vision, for the men who were with me did not see the vision, but a great trembling fell upon them, and they fled to hide themselves. So I was left alone and saw this great vision, and no strength was left in me; my radiant appearance was fearfully changed, and I retained no strength (10:4-9).*

On other occasions, while there was still a strange aspect to the appearance of the angelic visitors, they were not so terrifying as the one seen by Daniel:

♦ the angel who rolled back the stone from Christ's tomb was *"like lightning, and his raiment white as snow,"* yet the women were able to converse with him (Mt 28:2-6). However, a more terrible display of the angel's power and glory may have assaulted the soldiers who fainted.

♦ *Mark 16:5* describes the same angel simply as a young man in a white robe; but apparently to other eyes he seemed to be *"two men in dazzling apparel"* (Lu 24:4).

♦ when Mary looked in the tomb *"she saw two angels in white sitting where the body of Jesus had lain"*; obviously angels, but apparently not too terrible (Jn 20:12).

♦ the apostles saw two angels as *"two men in white robes"* (Ac 1:10); and to Cornelius the angel appeared as "a man in bright apparel" (Ac 10:30).

Which leads me on to say that more commonly, angels make themselves visible -

ii. With a natural shape

Frequently angels have appeared in such an ordinary human form onlookers failed to recognise them as supernatural visitors. It seems, for example, both Abraham and Lot failed to realise until later that their visitors were angels (Ge 18:2-8; 19:1- 8); and the same was true of Joshua (5:13), of Gideon (Jg 6:19- 22), and of Manoah (13:15-20).

We do well then to take careful notice of the advice given by the writer to the Hebrews -

> *Let brotherly love continue. Do not neglect to show hospitality to strangers, for thereby some have entertained angels unawares! (13:1-2).*

But that raises an obvious question: do angels in human form take on human flesh and other physical attributes, or are they merely insubstantial apparitions? The answer is uncertain. But Tertullian (circa 200) thought they did assume material properties. In an argument against the heretic Marcion (who denied that Jesus was a real flesh-and-blood man) Tertullian wrote -

> (You say that the angels) held intercourse with Abraham and Lot in a phantom state, that of merely putative flesh, and yet did truly converse, and eat, and work, as they had been commissioned to do ... (But) you must know that it will not be conceded to you, that in the angels there was only a putative flesh, but one of true and solid human substance. For if (on your terms) it was no difficulty to him to manifest true sensations and actions in a putative flesh, it was much more easy for him still to have assigned the true substance of flesh to these true sensations and actions ... (For he is) able to supply to angels too a flesh of any material whatsoever, who built even the world out of nothing, into so many and so various bodies, and that at a word!

> And really, if your god promises to men some time or other the true nature of angels (for he says, "They shall be like angels") why should not my God also have fitted on to angels the true substance of men, from whatever source derived? ... It is more difficult for God to practise deception than to produce real flesh from any material whatever, even without the means of birth ... (So the flesh of angels) was truly human flesh, and yet not born.

> It was truly human, because of the truthfulness of God, who can neither lie nor deceive, and because (angelic beings) cannot be dealt with by men in a

human way except in human substance ... (But) from whatever quarter they obtained it, and by what means soever they afterwards entirely divested themselves of it, they yet never pretended it to be unreal flesh ...

(Therefore) we can now recall to our own minds, and remind the heretics also, that he has promised that he will one day form men into angels, who once formed angels into men.[31]

Tertullian refers twice to *Luke 20:36*, where, however, Christ does not say that we shall become angels, but merely shall be like the angels (particularly in the loss of sexual distinctives). As for the rest of his argument, it was thought quite powerful in its own time, but modern readers may find it less convincing. Which does not mean his conclusions are wrong. It may well be true that angels, when they assume human shape also assume human substance.

b. They are Seen by the Saints

In the end, whether angels do take on material bodies when they appear on the earth, or only seem to, is futile to ask. All that can be said with certainty is they took on human form in the minds of those who saw them.

Some commentators claim that no angel ever appeared to a godless person, or that no wicked person was ever warned by an angel of impending danger. Good angels (they say) always appeared to good people. But is that really so? It could be argued that angels were seen by ungodly people in the cases of Balaam (Nu 22:31); the guards at the tomb (Mt 28:4); Saul (1 Sa 28:8-20); and the crowd in Jerusalem (Jn 12:28-30).

However, it is true to say, if angels have appeared to ungodly people such occasions have been rare. Overwhelmingly, angelic

---

[31]   Against Marcion, Bk 3, ch 9; Ante-Nicene Fathers, Vol 3, pg. 328,329.

visits have been to the children of God. The angels are sent primarily to minister to the servants of the Lord. They have, however, often been the unseen agents by whom God has inflicted punishment on the wicked. But I will discuss that below.

4. OTHER EXOTIC SHAPES

Apart from the seraphim, cherubim, and archangels, which I describe in Chapter Five, regular angels may appear in various exotic shapes - such as wheels, chariots, animals, and so on. See Ez 1:5-9; 8:2-3; Zc 1:8; 6:1-5; Re 4:6-8; etc.

Our study of the attributes of the angels is continued in your next chapter.

CHAPTER FOUR

MIGHTY HOST

Angels have talked with him, and shown him
thrones:
Ye knew him not; he was not one of ye,
Ye scorned him with an undiscerning scorn:
Ye could not read the marvel in his eye ...
Always there stood before him, night and day,
Of wayward vary coloured circumstance
The imperishable presences serene
Colossal, without form, or sense, or sound,
Dim shadows but unwaning presences
Fourfaced to four corners of the sky ...

- from "The Mystic," by Alfred, Lord Tennyson; 1830.

Tennyson's poem eulogises the mystic who keenly senses the reality of the spiritual dimension that everywhere surrounds us; the person who is constantly aware of the presence of the angels of God. It must surely be mightily encouraging, a great confidence-builder, to live with such an awareness. The psalmist spoke about it-

The angel of the Lord encamps around those who
fear him, and delivers them (Ps 34:7).

In this chapter we continue our study of the attributes of these encircling warriors -

I. VAST IN NUMBER

The scriptures delight in stating two things about the number of the angels: it is vast, yet limited. Man cannot number them; yet their number is known to God. Their prodigious tally shows the glory of the angels, so multitudinous in their host; but their finite ranks show the glory of God, who made and counted them all.

Of the original number of angels, only two thirds remain, for the angels who were drawn by Satan into rebellion against God comprised one third of the total -

> *Behold, a great red dragon ... his tail swept down a third of the stars of heaven, and cast them to the earth (Re 12:4).*

Assuming that verse does describe the banishment from heaven of the fallen angels, then the use of the expression *"one third"* discloses the finite and fixed number of the angels.

The loss of that one third has diminished the strength of the holy angels. Yet it remains true, for every evil angel warring against the servants of God there are at least two holy angels fighting for them!

Elisha was very confident of angelic protection when he encouraged his frightened servant: *"Fear not, for those who are with us are more that those who are with them!"* When the young man remained apprehensive, the prophet asked God to *"open his eyes that he may see!"* Then the Lord *"opened the eyes of the young man, and he saw; and behold, the mountain was full of horses and chariots of fire"* (2 Kg 6:15-17).

Great men of God, like Elisha, have always had a clear vision of the heavenly host, and they have found assurance in the knowledge of this mighty army of the Lord fighting on their behalf -

> *The Lord came from Sinai, and dawned from Seir upon us; he shone forth from Mount Paran, he came from the ten thousands upon thousands of holy ones, with flaming fire at his right hand (De 33:2).*

> *Dominion and fear are with God ... Is there any number to his armies? Upon whom does his light not arise? (Jb 25:2,3).*

With mighty chariotry, twice ten thousand, thousands upon thousands, the Lord came from Sinai into the holy place (Ps 68:17).

As I looked, thrones were placed and one that was ancient of days took his seat; his raiment was white as snow, and the hair of his head like pure wool; his throne was fiery flames, its wheels were burning fire. A stream of fire issued and came forth from before him; a thousand thousands served him, and ten thousand times ten thousand stood before him ... (Da 7:10).

You have come to Mount Zion and to the city of the living God, the heavenly Jerusalem, and to innumerable angels in festal gathering, and to the assembly of the first-born who are enrolled in heaven ... (He 12:22).

Then I looked, and I heard around the throne ... the voices of many angels, numbering myriads of myriads and thousands of thousands ... (Re 5:11).

These things are written in scripture for your benefit, to encourage you (as Elisha's servant was) by revealing the great host defending you. The warriors of the invincible God of Battle *(Ex 15:3) are standing at your side to contend with you against the powers of darkness!*

II. GLORIOUS IN HOLINESS

The unfallen angels are constantly portrayed in scripture as *"holy"* beings (Jb 5:1; 15:15; Da 8:13; Mk 8:38).

Holiness is a quality that can exist in four forms:

- ◆ Attributed
- ◆ Intrinsic

- ◆ Dynamic

- ◆ Absolute

A. THE FOUR KINDS OF HOLINESS

1. ABSOLUTE HOLINESS

Absolute holiness belongs only to God. This central fact about God's nature was hammered into Israel's consciousness over centuries of instruction and bitter experience -

> *Say to all the congregation of the people of Israel,*
> *"You shall be holy; for I the Lord your God am*
> *holy" (Le 19:2).*

They had to learn that the holiness of the Lord God is utterly uncompromising. He can never look on evil without avenging it; and men and women must encounter this holiness of God, and yield to it in awe, before they discover any other divine attribute. Indeed, no other attribute of God (his love, his grace, his kindness, and the like) can be truly known until you meet his holiness. *"The fear of God is the beginning of wisdom."*

Even the mighty seraphim who stand closest of all creatures to the shining throne of God devote themselves to celebrating and proclaiming his ineffable holiness -

> *One called to another and said: "Holy, holy, holy is*
> *the Lord of hosts; the whole earth is full of his*
> *glory." And the foundations of the thresholds shook*
> *at the voice of him who called, and the house was*
> *filled with smoke (Is 6:3- 4).*

John had a similar vision -

> *And the four living creatures, each of them with six*
> *wings, are full of eyes all round and within, and day*
> *and night they never cease to sing, "Holy, holy, holy*

is the Lord God Almighty, who was and is and is to come!" (Re 4:8).

Such absolute holiness is non-communicable; that is, it is a strictly divine attribute; it belongs to God alone and can never be given to angel, man, nor to any other creature. But God does convey aspects of his holiness to his creatures in one of its three other forms. Thus we move on to -

2. ATTRIBUTED HOLINESS

Attributed holiness belongs to people, nations, and things God has arbitrarily designated holy, either temporarily or permanently, in order to satisfy his own purpose; such as -

♦ he declared the tabernacle holy, along with all its furnishings and artifacts;

♦ a piece of ground or a certain location could be marked off as a holy place;

♦ a man performing a certain function could be treated as holy while he was fulfilling his duty; and so on.

The essence of attributed holiness is this: God imposes it solely by his own will, without reference to the personal desire or character of the thing he designates holy. Since attributed holiness depends entirely upon divine choice, it may be given or withdrawn by God at his pleasure.

3. INTRINSIC HOLINESS

Intrinsic holiness belongs to anything created by God as holy; that is, it is holy in its very nature and character, and that holiness cannot be withdrawn, not even by God.

Thus we say that the name of God and the word of God are intrinsically holy. Holiness belongs to their very essence, and they cannot be otherwise -

He sent redemption to his people; he has commanded his covenant for ever. Holy and terrible is his name! (Ps 111:9; see also Ps 105:3; 106:47; 145:21; etc).

4. DYNAMIC HOLINESS

Dynamic holiness belongs to the servants of God who, being free moral agents, have consciously chosen to emulate their God and to be holy as he is holy. They are made holy by God, or else he imputes holiness to them, in response to their own voluntary choice. Good and evil having been set before them, they have chosen righteousness instead of iniquity; holiness has therefore been wrought in them by their Lord. This is the kind of holiness we know who believe in Christ.

The question now arises, in which of those four meanings are the angels holy? They certainly do not possess absolute holiness, for that belongs to God alone. Nor can we say they possess merely attributed holiness. The scriptures speak of the angels in a way that shows their holiness must be thought of as indestructible, as essential to their very nature. (See Mt 25:31; Mk 8:38; Lu 9:26; 1 Th 3:13; Ju 14; Re 14:10).

Thus holiness must be seen as an integral part of their character; it arises from within them, it is not imposed from outside. So it must be either intrinsic or dynamic; and the latter would seem to be the case, for the following reasons -

B. CHOICE AND PROBATION

1. FREE MORAL AGENTS

God has apparently never created a rational being in whom holiness was compulsive, irresistible, involuntary. It would seem that intrinsic holiness properly belongs only to impersonal things such as the name or the word of God; but holiness in a rational or personal being is valuable to God only when it results from voluntary choice.

That the angels are free moral agents is made clear by the rebellion of some of them against God, for which they heard a dread penalty spoken against them -

> *God did not spare the angels when they sinned, but cast them into Tartarus and committed them to pits of nether gloom to be kept until the judgment ... The angels that did not keep their own position, but left their proper dwelling, have been kept by him in eternal chains in the nether gloom until the judgment of the great day (2 Pe 2:4; Ju 6).*

At some point after their creation the angels were evidently given an opportunity by God to choose obedience or disobedience to his will. A portion of them decided to reject the service of God. How could they be so stupid? How could they ever hope to succeed in a war against the Almighty? There must have been something about the choice facing them that made them confident they would prevail. Their hope was vain -

> *Now war arose in heaven, Michael and his angels fighting against the dragon. And the dragon and his angels fought back, but he was defeated, and there was no longer any place for them in heaven. And the great dragon was thrown down, that ancient serpent, who is called the devil and Satan, the deceiver of the whole world--he was thrown down to the earth, and his angels were thrown down with him. (Rev 12:7-9 ESV)*

Perhaps God hid from all the angels the full extent of his power, so that the choice to serve him would be made, not out of fear of his superior strength, but out of love. It seems unlikely that *"the great dragon and his angels"* would have declared war on God, and against Michael and his angels, unless they had believed there was some likelihood of victory. Perhaps only after their choice had been made did they discover the awful measure of their delusion and the inevitability of their defeat.

2. MORAL CHOICE INESCAPABLE

A choice such as this is essential for the development of true holiness within a rational and moral being. Man faces that choice. God could compel obedience by a terrifying display of his awful majesty and might. But he seeks a *"willing"* people, not just an obedient one; he wants us to serve him out of love, not out of fear -

> *Your people will offer themselves freely on the day you lead your host upon the holy mountains (Ps 110:3).*

Service from anything other than a willing, joyful, and loving heart is repulsive to God. The standard he desires is this -

> *Whoever is of a generous heart, let him bring the Lord's offering ... And they came, everyone whose heart stirred him, and everyone whose spirit moved him ... So they came, both men and women, all who were of a willing heart (Ex 35:3,21,22).*

And again:

> *If you are willing and obedient, you shall eat the good of the land; but if you refuse and rebel, you shall be devoured by the sword; for the mouth of the Lord has spoken (Is 1:19-20)*

That is why the question Moses presented to Israel continues to confront us -

> *See, I have set before you this day life and good, death and evil ... I call heaven and earth to witness against you this day, that I have set before you life and death, blessing and curse; therefore choose life,*

that you ... may live, loving the Lord your God,
obeying his voice, and cleaving to him (De
30:15,19-20).

When he presents us with that choice, God reveals enough of his
true nature and power to leave the rebellious without excuse (Ro
1:18-22); but not enough to negate moral freedom, nor to
overwhelm love by compulsion.

The angels, like man, were created free moral agents; but until that
morality was put to the test it remained neutral and unrealised.
They were made with a capacity for holiness, but that capacity lay
dormant until an exercise of moral choice either awakened or
destroyed it. So a time of testing came upon the angels. Who would
be on the Lord's side? Michael and the greater part of the angels
chose to serve the Lord God. Lucifer and his angels chose to
declare war on heaven. Holiness at once became the primary
character of the first, and wickedness of the second.

3. A TIME OF PROBATION

a. For the Angels

Paul speaks of the *"elect"* angels (1 Ti 5:21), which implies that
the holy angels once served a time of probation, to prove
themselves worthy to be the servants of God. Since they chose to
cleave to the Lord, and won their way to divine election, holiness
in its dynamic form is now presumably an immutable part of their
nature. There is no longer any possibility of them refusing the
loving service of God. By their own deep choice, dynamic holiness
is now fixed in them for ever.

The early church firmly believed that the angels were put to the test
after their creation -

> God created both angels and men free to do that
> which is righteous, and he appointed periods of time
> during which he knew it would be good for them to

have the exercise of free will. (Justin Martyr, Dialogue With Trypho, 102)

Those who were foreknown to be unrighteous, whether men or angels, are not wicked by God's fault, but each ... by his own fault is what he will appear to be ... God, wishing men and angels to follow his will, resolved to create them free to do righteousness, possessing reason ... and with a law that they should be judged by him, if they do anything contrary to right reason. (Ibid., 140,141)

Just as with men, who have freedom of choice as to both virtue and vice ... so is it among the angels. Some, free agents, you will observe, such as they were created by God, continued in those things for which God made them and over which he had ordained them; but some outraged both the constitution of their nature and the government entrusted to them ... [32]

Nor are we to suppose that it is the result of accident that a particular office is assigned to a particular angel ... For we are not to imagine that they obtained these offices otherwise than by their own merits, and by the zeal and excellent qualities which they severally displayed before this world was formed ... (those offices) were conferred by God, the just and impartial Ruler of all things, agreeably to the merits and good qualities and mental vigour of each individual spirit.[33]

---

[32]   Athenagoras, A Plea For Christians, 24.

[33]   Origen, *Principles*, Bk. 1, ch. 8; Ante-Nicene Fathers, Vol. Four.

b. For Christians

Our experience parallels that of the angels. We look forward with eager longing to that coming day, when the choice we made to serve God will have been sufficiently tested in the fiery crucible of life. Then our election in Christ will be confirmed, and the principle of holiness within us will be eternally established. Sin will then be inconceivable. We shall no longer be at risk of falling away from the love of God. Holiness will not be merely attributed to us; it will be the dynamic centre of our very existence.

Attributed holiness has no influence on character or destiny; intrinsic holiness is morally neutral and spiritually static; but dynamic holiness, resulting from free choice, is morally powerful, spiritually creative, personally satisfying, and filled with potential for growth in the life, love, and service of God.

That is the quality of holiness held by redeemed man and by the unfallen angels.

III. SPLENDID IN WORSHIP

A. WORSHIP IS THEIR GREATEST JOY

The surpassing joy of the angels, and their most noble endeavour, is the worship and praise of the Lord God -

> *The morning stars sang together, and all the sons of God shouted for joy (Jb 38:7).*

> *You alone are the Lord ... and the multitudes of heaven worship you (Ne 9:6).*

> *Ascribe to the Lord, O heavenly beings, ascribe to the Lord glory and strength. Ascribe to the Lord the glory of his name; worship the Lord in holy array (Ps 29:1-2).*

One (seraph) called to another and said, "Holy, holy, holy is the Lord of hosts; the whole earth is full of his glory" (Is 6:3).

There was with the angel a multitude of the heavenly host praising God and saying, "Glory to God in the highest, and on earth peace among men ... !" (Lu 2:14).

Day and night (the angels) never cease to sing,

"Holy, holy, holy is the Lord God Almighty, who was, and is, and is to come!" (Re 4:8).

I heard around the throne ... the voice of many angels ... and I heard every creature in heaven ... saying, "To him who sits upon the throne and to the Lamb be blessing and honour and glory and might for ever and ever!" (5:11-13) .

All the angels stood around the throne ... and they fell on their faces before the throne and worshipped God, saying, "Amen! Blessing and glory and wisdom and thanksgiving and honour and power and might be to our God for ever and ever! Amen!" (7:11-12).

The holiest and mightiest of the host of heaven delight to worship the Lord God day and night, and to gather with joyful praise around his high and kingly throne. No wonder scripture demands that we too should worship the Lord continually, and in the beauty of holiness. Man stands tallest when he is kneeling before the throne of God.

B. WORSHIP IS THEIR GREATEST EXAMPLE

Scripture calls us to emulate the angels in just two respects: their holy obedience to God; their unfailing worship of God. The one cannot exist without the other. Worship is unacceptable without obedience. Obedience is impossible apart from worship. They gain strength and glory from each other. Both ideas occupy an exquisite statement in the prophecy of Jeremiah -

> *A glorious throne set on high from the beginning is*
> *the place of our sanctuary (17:12).*

The prophet was speaking primarily about the Temple in Jerusalem. He was urging the people to reverence their holy *"sanctuary"*, to call it in truth the house of God, the place of divine worship. If they would do so, then God himself would establish it as *"a glorious throne set on high"*, indestructible, victorious, the guarantee that Israel would triumph for ever.

But if the people betrayed their worship, if they despised God, then their glorious throne, their high sanctuary, would be ruthlessly overthrown, and they also would perish in its fall. So Jeremiah warned them -

> *O Lord, the hope of Israel, all who forsake thee*
> *shall be put to shame; those who turn away from*
> *thee shall be written in the earth, for they have*
> *forsaken the Lord, the Fountain of living water (vs.*
> *13).*

Written in earth! A name marked by a finger in the dust, then erased by nothing more than a careless zephyr. A people without permanence, without hope, whose only prospect is irretrievable ruin. Put to shame because they forsook the Rock from which they had been hewn. Desolated with endless thirst because they scorned the Fountain of living water.

For us, the sense of the passage is simply that our defence and our victory lies in worship. Although we have no sanctuary fixed in a building, our bodies are now the temples of the Holy Spirit. Our sanctuary, our place of worship, is within us. We create that sanctuary, wherever we are, whenever we heartily worship the Lord our God.

True worship instantly causes your *"sanctuary"* to become *"a glorious throne set on high"*, invincible, holy, filled with the presence of the Lord. Possessing that divine fullness you will be able to sing with Jeremiah,

> *Heal me, O Lord, and I shall be healed; save me, and I shall be saved; for thou art my praise! (vs. 14).*

Total salvation! Complete healing! That double grace flows out of the high throne of God, that is, out of worship - for praise becomes a glorious palace in which the Lord will take his seat and from which he stretches out his hand to save to the uttermost those who trust in him.

The Psalmist made the same discovery -

> *Thou art holy, enthroned on the praises of Israel. In thee our fathers trusted; they trusted and thou didst deliver them. To thee they cried and were saved; in thee they trusted and were not disappointed (Ps 22:3-5).*

Worship places man on high; it becomes for him a precious pedestal; it sets him in the heavenlies with Christ; it creates a place of sanctuary; it transforms him into an eternal son of God; it causes the Lord to become his refuge and his strong right arm; it allies him with the hosts of angels; it lifts him into a new dimension; it draws him on to fulfil the destiny appointed for him by God.

IV. POWERFUL IN SERVICE

A. THE ANGELS ARE STRONG

Angels have superhuman power, but their strength falls far short of God's. They are not omnipotent. There are many things they cannot do, and there are times when, to accomplish the will of God, they have to exert all their strength against the enemy. Success for them is not always easy.

1. MIGHTY STRENGTH

The most striking characteristic of the angels is their mighty strength. They also possess beauty and intelligence; but in scripture, descriptions of their immense power overwhelm those attributes -

> *Give unto the Lord, O ye mighty, give unto the Lord glory and strength (Ps 29:1, KJV).*

> *God standeth in the congregation of the mighty; he judgeth among the gods (Ps 82:1, KJV).*

> *Bless the Lord, O you his angels, you mighty ones who do his word (Ps 103:20).*

Paul describes the angels exclusively in terms of power -

> *... thrones, dominions, principalities, authorities (Cl 1:16) ... The Lord Jesus (will be) revealed from heaven with his mighty angels in flaming fire, inflicting vengeance upon those who do not know God and upon those who do not obey the gospel of our Lord Jesus Christ (2 Th 1:7- 8).*

What strength angels have! Forces that are utterly destructive to man leave them unaffected. Hence the fiercest flame cannot touch them, and they are able to impart this same immunity from harm to us who believe -

> *... the angel of the Lord ascended in the flame ... I see four men loose, walking in the midst of the fire, and they are not hurt, and the appearance of the fourth is like a son of the gods (Jg 13:20; Da 3:25).*

Great power remains the primary characteristic of even the fallen angels, except that now the power is corrupt and hideous -

... the prince of this world ... a strong man armed ... powers of darkness ... the great dragon ... a roaring lion ... principalities, powers, the world rulers of this present darkness, spiritual hosts of wickedness ... the prince of the power of the air ... etc ...

By the power of his mighty angels, the Lord smote the first- born of Egypt, confused the army of Syria, annihilated the army of Assyria, closed the mouths of lions, shook the earth, and wrought great signs and wonders. There is no reason to suppose he is not doing the same today.

2. MEASURED STRENGTH

The strength of the angels is not limitless. Some things lie utterly beyond their power, and others they can accomplish only with difficulty. The psalmist is emphatic -

Let the heavens praise thy wonders, O Lord, thy faithfulness in the assembly of the holy ones! For who in the skies can be compared to the Lord? Who among the heavenly beings is like the Lord, a God feared in the council of the holy ones, great and terrible above all that are round about him? O Lord God of hosts, who is mighty as thou art, O Lord, with thy faithfulness round about thee? (Ps 89:5-8).

There is also Daniel's remarkable passage, which tells how one of the angels of God had to struggle for twenty one days against a demon (*"the prince of the kingdom of Persia"*). Even with the help of the great archangel Michael the battle was hardly won - see 10:2-21.

Centuries before the time of Daniel, Michael engaged in another conflict, this time with Satan himself, and he had to acknowledge that he could prevail only with divine assistance (Ju 9).

Therefore the holy angels temper their strength with meekness. Pride is abhorrent to them, for they know that arrogance is a snare laid by the dread Enemy of God. Their meekness is an example for us to follow, and those who refuse to do so are thrust under the anger of God -

> *The Lord knows how to ... keep the unrighteous under punishment until the day of judgment, and especially those who ... despise authority. Bold and wilful, they are not afraid to revile the glorious ones, whereas angels, though greater in might and power, do not pronounce a reviling judgment upon them before the Lord (2 Pe 2:9-11; see also Ju 8-9).*

B. THE ANGELS ARE WISE

1. A VAST KNOWLEDGE

The woman of Tekoa flattered King David by saying he had *"wisdom like the wisdom of the angel of God to know all things that are in the earth"* (2 Sa 14:20). Her statement reflected a popular belief among the Jews about the superior wisdom of the angels. Jewish legends perpetuated many notions about angelic wisdom. For example:

♦ that Noah learned herbal lore and the art of medicine from the angels;

♦ that Gabriel taught Moses the story of Creation and other details about the early history of man;

♦ that the other patriarchs of Israel also gained their wisdom by the mediation of angels.

The *Apocrypha* declares that Azazel taught men various scientific arts, while an angel assured Tobit he was familiar with all that was happening in the world.

2. A LIMITED KNOWLEDGE

Such popular beliefs about the immense wisdom of the angels is generally confirmed in scripture. But angels are clearly denied omniscience; there is a definite limit placed on their knowledge and understanding. The mysteries of the future, the secrets of our redemption, the purposes of God, these things are known to them only insofar as the Lord himself gives them revelation.

One of the sayings of Christ shows that while the knowledge possessed by angels is prodigious it is also finite. Referring to the time of his return, he said -

> *Of that day and hour no one knows, not even the angels of heaven, nor the Son, but the Father only (Mt 24:36; see also Mk 13:32).*

That saying implies first, the angels possess knowledge far beyond that of man; but second, there are some things they do not know. Among the matters hidden from the angels are at least some future events, and at least some of the mysteries of our redemption. Peter, for example, implies that angels cannot penetrate the deeper secrets of the gospel-

> *The good news (was preached) to you through the Holy Spirit sent from heaven, things into which angels long to look (1 Pe 1:12).*

And Paul says that the angels are able to learn about the wisdom of God by observing the church (Ep 3:10).

3. A PERSONAL KNOWLEDGE

If the angels are wise, then three things follow: they are personal, intelligent, voluntary.

Wisdom has no meaning apart from intelligence; every intelligent being must also be personal; an intelligent personal being must also have the power of voluntary action. Angels therefore are not mindless automatons; nor are they identical robots. The angels bear individual names; they have a different appearance; they have different personalities; they are able to search for knowledge and to learn; they have freedom of choice and a significant degree of freedom of action.

The Bible names Gabriel and Michael, and depicts them as different from each other in character. It tells their great wisdom and power, and shows them exercising choice in their actions.

One of the chief marks of personality in the angels (as it is in man) is their ability to communicate with each other and with people. Since angels talk, they must be personal and intelligent beings -

> *The angel who talked with me said to me, "I will show you what they are" (Zc 1:9; see also 1:14; 4:5; 5:10; 6:4; etc.).*

The angel who conversed with John (Re 21:9,15; 22:1,6) obviously associated himself with John, thus demonstrating that human nature and angelic nature are similar in many points -

> *I am a fellow servant with you and with your brethren the prophets (22:9).*

It appears that angels and men share the same basic characteristics of personality, intelligence, and voluntary choice.

4. A HUMBLE KNOWLEDGE

Though angels have superhuman intelligence, they do not, unlike proud man or the fallen angels, disdain obedience. On the contrary, it is their humble joy to serve God -

> *Bless the Lord, all his hosts, his ministers that do his will (Ps 103:20).*

The words of the Lord's prayer (Mt 6:10) imply that the heavenly multitude obey the Father with gladness. The more vast their wisdom, the more wholeheartedly they serve. How they indict man, who though his wisdom is so much less, yet puffs himself up with pride when he has gained a little knowledge, thinking he can now dispense with religion and God!

5. A DEPENDENT KNOWLEDGE

With all their wisdom and might the angels are still wholly dependent upon God. Their strength and knowledge is his gift to them, and without his active help they cannot complete the work he has given them to do. In this also, their position is similar to ours.

God, by contrast, is not dependent upon the angels. He may act with or without their agency. They are not free from error, and there may be times when angelic involvement would hinder rather than help the divine purpose.

a. Not Infallible

Eliphaz tells about a chilling experience he had one night, when an angelic spirit glided past his face, making the hair on his flesh stand up, and transfixing him with fright. When the spirit stood still, Eliphaz could see its dim form, but he could not discern its appearance. Then it spoke -

> *Can mortal man be righteous before God? Can a man be pure before his Maker? Even in his servants he puts no trust, and his angels he charges with error; how much more those who dwell in houses of clay ... ? (Jb 4:12-19).*

Absolute infallibility belongs only to God; it does not belong either to angel or man. Eliphaz was so sure about this (especially after that midnight visitation), he repeated the lesson -

> *Behold, God puts no trust in his holy ones, and the heavens are not clean in his sight (15:15).*

> *The angels were all created by God and Christ, for the service of the Godhead; and he who created them can readily dispense with them -*

Thou art the Lord, thou alone; thou hast made heaven, the heaven of heavens, with all their host ... and the host of heaven worships thee (Ne 9:6; see also Ph 2:9-11; Cl 1:16; He 1:6).

b. Not Irrelevant

But if the angels are not necessary, if they are dependent, why did God create them? Why does he bother to use them? Why clutter the universe with irrelevant agents?

To such questions there is no final answer, any more than there is to similar questions about man. But with caution, lest the glory of God be even slightly diminished, perhaps I could say that angels and men are both in some way necessary to God, and not merely contingent upon a divine whim. There are indications that God finds delight in his creation. He enjoys conveying infinite pleasure and satisfaction to his servants by permitting them to become his agents and to do his will.

Though God's absolute autonomy cannot be circumscribed in any way, yet perhaps creation is an essential part of his identity as Creator; hence it is his yen to create and to pronounce good the work of his hands. Then having created, he guides his creation to find fulfilment through joyfully praising his everlasting glory. That is the gist of Paul's opening remarks to the Ephesians -

(God) chose us in (Christ) before the foundation of the world, that we should be holy and blameless before him. He destined us in love to be his sons through Jesus Christ, according to the purpose of his will, to the praise of his glorious grace which he freely bestowed on us in the Beloved ... In him, according to the purpose of him who accomplishes all things according to the counsel of his will, we who first hoped in Christ have been destined and appointed to live for the praise of his glory ... until

we acquire possession of (our inheritance), to the
praise of his glory (Ep 1:4-6, 11-12, 14).

Thus God's chief end in creating you and me was to bring us fulfilment and happiness; but we find our chief happiness in living for the praise of God's glory.

I suggest the same kind of reciprocity may exist between God and his angels.

But whether creation is a necessary act of God, or is simply contingent upon his will, is a question beyond present solution. In the meantime, I rejoice because I am made, because I am redeemed, and because I am free to serve God in the fullness of his Spirit. That happiness I share with the angels, and I am sure they delight to share it with me!

V. MYSTERIOUS IN BEING

A. ANGELS ARE DIFFERENT

Jesus declared that angels are a separate class of being from mankind (in particular, they lack any innate sexual distinction). See Mt 22:30; Lu 20:34-36; Mk 12:25. Those sayings lead to certain conclusions -

1. THE ANGELS ARE REAL

Against the opinions of the Sadducees, who denied both the resurrection and the existence of angels, Jesus affirmed his belief in both -

> These words were spoken by our Lord in response
> to the doubts of the Sadducees on the subject of the
> resurrection. Christ's reply is in effect this: The
> source of your error is that you do not fully
> recognise the power of God. You seem to think that
> God can make only one kind of body, with one sort

of functions, and dependent on one means of life. In that way you limit unduly the power of God. "In that age" (Lu 20:35), "when they rise from the dead" (Mk 12:25), men do not eat and drink (Ro 14:17). Not being mortal, they are not dependent on food for nourishment, nor have they, by nature, sensuous appetites, but they are "equal to the angels".

Thus skilfully did Jesus give a double-edged reply to the teachings of the Sadducees (Ac 23:8). While answering their objection against the resurrection, he affirms that "those who are accounted worthy to attain to that age, and to the resurrection from the dead ... are equal to the angels" - thus plainly disclosing his belief in angels and setting it over against their disbelief ...

The Rabbis interpreted Da 7:10 to teach that the nature of the angels is fire. "They are nourished by the radiance which streams from the presence of God. They need no material nourishment, and their nature is not responsive to bodily pleasures" ... They are also said to be "spiritual beings" ... "without sensuous requirements" ... "without hatred, envy, or jealousy."[34]

2. BOTH ALIKE AND UNLIKE

Note the differences and similarities between us and the angels. At present we are sensual, material, hungry, and subject to death; whereas angels are none of those things. But in the resurrection we shall become equal to the angels; which means that sexual

---

[34] Dictionary of Christ and the Gospels; edited by James Hastings; Vol. 1, pg. 54, article *Angels*; Baker Book House, Grand Rapids, Michigan; 1973 reprint.

differences will vanish, carnal appetite will be no more, physical barriers will no longer restrain us, and death will be banished for ever.

B. ANGELS ARE ASEXUAL

Christ affirmed the lack of sexuality in angels. They are neither male nor female. This angelic asexuality seems to preclude the traditional idea that Ge 6:4 describes an unholy union between fallen angels and women.

That tradition was popular among both the Jews and the early Christians -

> Some (of the angels) continued in those things for which God had made them, and over which he had ordained them; but some outraged both the constitution of their nature and the government entrusted to them ... (and) fell into impure love of virgins, and were subjugated by the flesh ... Of these lovers of virgins, therefore, were begotten those who are called giants ...

> These angels, then, who have fallen from heaven, and haunt the air and the earth ... (along with) the souls of the giants, which are the demons who wander about the world, perform actions similar; the one (that is, the demons) to the natures they have received, the other (that is, the angels) to the appetites they have indulged.[35]

And a much earlier Jewish work, dated around the first century B.C., retells the Genesis story -

---

[35]   Athenagoras, *A Plea For Christians*, 24,25; Ante-Nicene Fathers, Vol. Two.

> In those days, when the children of men had multiplied, it happened that there were born unto them handsome and beautiful daughters. And the angels, the children of heaven, saw them and desired them; and they said to one another, "Come, let us choose wives for ourselves from the among the daughters of man and beget us children" ... And the women became pregnant and gave birth to great giants whose heights were 300 cubits ...[36]

On the face of it, while that ancient tradition is still widely believed, it does seem highly improbable. It is even more improbable as an explanation of the origin of demons - but you will find more about that in my book on *Demonology*.

On the same matter, another commentator has written -

> The Jewish legends which interpret Ge 6:4 as teaching a commingling of angels with women, so as to produce "mighty men, men of renown", seems at variance with the above belief as to the immunity of celestial intelligences from all passion. It is true that Jude 6 and Enoch 15:3-7 both speak of the angels as having first "left their habitation" in heaven, but the fact that they were deemed capable of sexual intercourse implies a much coarser conception of the angelic nature than is taught in the words of our Lord, (and of the better Jewish teachers).[37]

---

[36]   *1 Enoch 6:1 - 7:2*; Charlesworth, Vol. One, pg. 15,16.

[37]   Hastings, op. cit

CONCLUSION

When the resurrection occurs, we will become products of a creative act similar to that by which God called the angels into being.

As I have suggested above, God formed all the angels together, in a moment of time, by one awesome fiat, and their number, nature, and identity are now fixed for ever (except for those who fell before their probation was ended).

Thus will it be in the resurrection.

The saints will leap from their graves to be at once transformed, in the twinkling of an eye, into the new-born sons of God. Morality and corruptibility will be gone for ever. They will be fashioned into the magnificent likeness of Christ. Their number, their nature, their identity, like that of the angels, will be fixed to change no more. They will truly be *"as the angels of God in heaven"*.

It is not careless of scripture to refer alike to angels and saints as *"the sons of God"* (Jb 1:6; 2:1; 38:7; Ho 1:10; Ro 8:19; 1 Jn 3:1-2). The angels are creatures whose nature combines both human and divine characteristics. In the resurrection we shall become like them, by our assumption of their divine attributes, and by shedding those aspects of our present humanity that are foreign to the heavenly realm.

But mark it once more: to become *"like"* an angel, even "equal" to one, is not the same as actually becoming an angel. Just as the present dissimilarities do not prevent a bond from existing between angelic and human nature, so the similarities we shall gain in the resurrection will not prevent us from remaining a separate species.

Some things that are ours now, the angels already share; and some things that are theirs now, we shall share in the resurrection. But angels will never become men; and men will never become angels.

CHAPTER FIVE

A SPLENDID HIERARCHY

I saw the Lord sitting on his throne, and all the host of heaven standing on his right hand and on his left (2 Ch 18:18).

THE GLORIOUS REALM ABOVE

There is an awesome mystery, a stupendous majesty, in heaven. It transcends our comprehension. The Lord God Almighty, the Ruler of the heavens, the earth, and all that is in them, has such servants at his command and such splendours surrounding his throne that mortal eye, even when granted a vision of heaven's marvels, cannot truly describe what it has seen. Our God controls a vast panoply of beings, powers, worlds, of which we humans gain only occasional glimpses.

Try to sense the overwhelming awe, the eerie feeling of being in the presence of the utterly unfamiliar, the stunning realisation of the sheer vastness of the Lord God's power and wisdom, that Zechariah must have felt when this vision came to him -

> *I saw in the night, and behold, a man riding upon a red horse! He was standing among the myrtle trees in the glen; and behind him were red, sorrel, and white horses. Then I said, "What are these my Lord?" The angel who talked with me said to me ... "These are they whom the Lord has sent to patrol the earth" ... And they answered the angel of the Lord ... "We have patrolled the earth, and behold, all the earth remains at rest" ... And again I lifted my eyes and saw, and behold four chariots came out from between two mountains; and the mountains were mountains of bronze. The first chariot had red*

horses, the second black horses ... When the steeds
came out, they were impatient to get off and patrol
the earth. And he said, "Go, patrol the earth." So
they patrolled the earth ... (Zc 1:7-11; 6:1-8;

See also the visions of Ezekiel, 1:4-28; 8:1-4; 10:1-22; and the visions of John, Re 4:1-11; 5:11-14).

There is a dimension beyond our own; there is a universe outside of the one in which we live; there is an angelic world, complex and glorious, ruled by the Lord God, parallel to ours, yet apart from it. From that sphere the angels have free access to our world, while we rarely penetrate the barriers between us and the realm of spirits.

SYMBOLS OF REALITY

Undoubtedly, many of these visionary experiences deal with symbols rather than with reality. For example, as awesome as the four horsemen and their chariots may have been to Zechariah, it is unlikely that red, sorrel, grey, and white horses exist in heaven. Those creatures were probably an angelic manifestation, strange, mysterious, powerful, fearful. They appeared in the form of chariots and horsemen simply to reveal the particular mission God had given them upon the earth.

The special value the vision has for us is its revelation of a dimension in the government of God ordinarily hidden from our eyes. For just as those angel servants of God patrolled the earth in Zechariah's day, scripture shows they are still doing so, and with the same effect.

Now that introduces the idea of various kinds and ranks of angels, which is the subject of this chapter -

I. AN ANCIENT BELIEF

A. COURTIERS AND CHOIRS

1. THE NINE CHOIRS

(Death) rounds the air, and breaks the hymnic notes
In birds', heaven's choristers, organic throats,
Which (if they did not die) might seem to be
A tenth rank in the heavenly hierarchy.[38]

Those lines are part of John Donne's bitter reproach of Death, which had cruelly cut off in the beauty of her youth the charming and virtuous Cecilia Boulstred. She was the daughter of his friend the Countess of Bedford. She died, apparently of melancholy, in 1609, aged twenty-five.

The poem is emotionally wrenching; but our present interest in it lies in Donne's reference to "a tenth rank in the heavenly hierarchy." He suggests that the birds, if Death would vanish, could be added to the nine choirs of angels that were popularly thought to exist. You may recall reading about those nine choirs in Chapter One, where you will also find the names of the Seven Archangels, along with other matters of popular legend.

A 5th-century work called The Heavenly Hierarchy (once thought to have been written by Dionysius of Athens, but now anonymous) established the division of the angelic host into nine choirs. The work was enormously influential upon the medieval church, until the Reformers denounced it. However, its imagery remained embedded in western culture, and the choirs continued to find their way into literature and art. To Donne's reference could be added others from Dante, Milton, and many more.

---

[38]   John Donne, *Elegy on Mistress Boulstred*; op. cit., pg. 249; lines 17-20.

Why has that idea been so enduring? Why is the idea of angelic ranks so appealing?

2. A ROYAL COURT

From earliest times people have been disposed to believe in angels; they naturally felt there should be a correspondence between the structures of the kingdom of God in heaven and the kingdoms of men on earth. If God is King, then he must have a kingdom and servants in divers ranks. A lone king, a king without a court, was inconceivable to the ancients. That is the sense of the verse which begins this chapter. The King is on his throne, and on either side stand his courtiers. He is an Absolute Monarch, his will is irresistible, and his servants are there to do his bidding.

But how much of that is truly endorsed by scripture?

B. ANGELS IN SCRIPTURE

The OT does not give any definition to the hierarchy of angels; in fact it hardly does more than hint the existence of such echelons. That silence, as we have seen, did not inhibit later Jews from formulating various ideas about the subject, which by the time of Christ had developed into an elaborate tradition. Specific titles were given to each rank, along with names for individual angels, and a multitude of other details.

Perhaps surprisingly, the NT writers generally appear to have adopted the Judaic tradition, although they did avoid the wilder speculations of their contemporaries. So the NT does give a clearer picture than the OT of the angelic hierarchy, and this NT ranking of the angels loosely reflects the popular Jewish belief.

Suggestions of an angelic hierarchy are given in Ro 8:38; 1 Co 15:24; Ep 1:21; 3:10; 6:12; Cl 1:16; 2:10,15; 1 Th 4:16; 1 Pe 3:22; 2 Pe 2:10. In the language of the RSV, those verses yield the following categories (not necessarily in order of importance):

- angels

- archangels

- principalities (rulers)

- powers

- authorities

- thrones

- dominions

To those seven categories some early Christians added the seraphim and cherubim, which then became the famous "nine choirs of angels".

A more cautious approach is preferable. There is no valid basis for supposing the apostles were attempting to give even an accurate, let alone a comprehensive, list of the various ranks in the angelic hierarchy. It is more reasonable to suppose they simply accepted the popular fancy that such a hierarchy did exist, and they used a more or less general collection of nouns to express the idea. The only grouping of angels (and the only order of precedence) that has any substantive support in the NT (and that only because it is most often used) is the following-

- rulers *(archai)*

- authorities *(exousiai)*

- powers *(dunameis)*

But even there the order of precedence is determined more by the strength of the nouns used than by any revealed heavenly order. It is unlikely the apostles related each of those nouns to a particular group of angels; more likely, they simply chose from the Greek language words that were expressive of rank. At any rate, I am not persuaded that rulers, authorities, powers have the same concrete sense as, say, archangels, seraphim, and cherubim. The latter are generic nouns, they refer to particular kinds of angels; but the former convey only a broad sense of hierarchy in the heavenlies.

Such caution finds encouragement in the refusal of the apostles to adopt either a set number of ranks or a set order. Thus groups like the following are found in their letters:

- ♦ angels, rulers, powers
- ♦ rulers, authorities, powers
- ♦ thrones, lordships, rulers, authorities
- ♦ rulers authorities
- ♦ angels authorities, powers

Such a lack of precision surely suggests the apostles had no more idea than we do just how many ranks there are in the angelic hierarchy, nor in what order those ranks should be listed.

However, precision is not entirely lacking. Some things can be affirmed about the hierarchy -

II. A COURT, A COUNCIL, AND AN ARMY

Once again Origen shows his caution (and agrees with what I have written above), by declaring that the grades of angels are many but indeterminate -

> We find in holy scripture numerous names of certain orders and offices, not only of holy beings, but also of those of an opposite description ... There are certain angels of God whom Paul terms "ministering spirits" ... We also find him designating them, from some unknown source, as thrones, and dominions, and principalities, and powers; and after this enumeration, as if knowing that there were still other ... orders beside those which he had named (he says that Christ is) "above all principal-

ity, and power, and might, and dominion, and every name that is named, not only in this world, but also in that which is to come." From which he shows that there were certain beings besides those which he had mentioned ... and that there were others which may not be named in this world, but will be named in the world to come.[39]

However, while we should refrain from setting up fixed ranks of angels, the scriptures do convey a vivid image of a hierarchy in heaven. A picture emerges of -

A. A HEAVENLY COURT

The angels form a royal court gathered around the throne of God in heaven - see 1 Kg 22:19; Da 7:9-10; Re 5:11; 7:11.

The picture given is exactly that of an Oriental monarch seated upon his royal throne, with his attendants, courtiers, advisers, guardians, and the like, standing before the throne and on either side. Closest to the throne are the throne-guardians, then those who are the throne-carriers, then the chief princes of the realm, then the highest government officials, and so on, each lesser rank standing a little further from the throne.

Notice the parallels between 1 Kg 22:10 & 19. In both cases, the earthly and the heavenly, the monarch is sitting upon his throne surrounded by his attendants. This is the heavenly scene -

- ◆ the throne-guardians of heaven, the seraphim, are placed closest to the throne of God (Is 6:1-3);

- ◆ also near, indeed supporting and carrying the throne, are the cherubim (Ez 10:18-19; 1:26-28; Re 4:6-11);

---

[39]   Op. cit., Bk 1, ch 5, sec 1.

- seated around the throne are the twenty-four chief councillors (Re 4:4);

- before the throne are seven high angels, perhaps identical with "the chief princes" mentioned by Daniel, and perhaps including Michael and Gabriel in their number (Da 10:13; Re 8:2);

- and then surrounding them all, a multitude of other majestic and glorious servants of the living God (Re. 5:11).[40]

As I have mentioned before, it is impossible to say to what degree these descriptions of the heavenly court should be taken literally. They undoubtedly represent reality; but just as certainly the language depicting that reality must be at least partly figurative. Hence it is unwise to be dogmatic about the number of ranks, their nature, and the like. Yet the real picture remains clear: heaven is organised on the pattern of a court around a throne, with gradations of dignity, power, and function.

Yet all is not flawless. With some temerity, the psalmist suggests that the angels may be less than perfect in their administration of the affairs of the kingdom of God -

> *God has taken his place in the divine council; in the midst of the gods he holds judgment: How long will you judge unjustly and show partiality to the wicked? (Ps 82:1-2; and see also 58:1-2.).*

They are sons of God, brilliant courtiers around the Father's throne, commissioned to act as his governors upon the earth, yet they may

---

[40] Some commentators identify "the living creatures" and "the twenty-four elders" with the saints; that is, they are not angels, but symbolic representations of the raptured church. I accept that they are angels; although I allow they may still portray symbolically the ultimate destiny of the saints, to be exalted to the highest glory and to stand closest of all to the throne of God.

be at fault. In the end, perfect justice, true infallibility, exists only in God himself (82:8; 58:11).[41]

The throne carriers of God are the cherubim, who hold a position of exalted honour in the royal court -

> *(God) rode on a cherub, and flew; he came swiftly upon the wings of the wind ... Thou who art enthroned upon the cherubim, shine forth ... God sits enthroned upon the cherubim (Ps 18:10; 80:1; 99:1; etc.)*

And the Revelator saw the seven Angels of the Presence, like seven flaming lamps burning, the seven spirits of God, standing in front of the throne - a position reserved in an oriental monarchy for those only of the most glorious rank (Re 4:5).

B. A HEAVENLY COUNCIL

> In the OT the angels are spoken of as forming "a council": e.g. in Ps 89:7 where God is said to be "very terrible in the council of the holy ones"; and in Ps 82:1, where he is said to "judge amidst the Elohim". This idea was a great favourite with later Jews, who maintained that "God does nothing without consulting the family above" ... To the same circle of ideas belong the words of the Lord Jesus: "Everyone that shall confess me before men, him

---

[41] An alternative view would equate the "gods" in those two psalms as the fallen angels, who are now banished from the Lord's service and face his furious judgment. Then there is no suggestion of the holy angels coming short of perfection in their service. But it is difficult to see how absolute perfection can belong to any creature, either in wisdom, skill, or achievement. Infallibility presumably belongs to God alone. If the angels are restricted in their abilities, and if they serve God as voluntary and intelligent agents, then they can make mistakes. But if that seems too startling, then be content to accept that the psalmist was talking about either fallen angels, or perhaps, by an extravagant simile, about corrupt earthly judges.

will the Son of man confess before the angels of God; but he that denieth me in the presence of men shall be denied in the presence of the angels of God" (Lu 12:8,9). Evidently the angels are interested spectators of men's behaviour, responsive to their victories and defeats, their sins and struggles; and we are here taught that to be denied before such a vast responsive assembly intensifies the remorse of the apostate, as to be confessed before them intensifies the joy of those who are "faithful unto death".

Again, in many courts, and particularly in that of the Persians, there were secretaries or scribes, whose business it was to keep a "book of records" (Es 6:1), in which the names and deeds of those who had deserved well of the king were honourably recorded. The metaphor of heaven as a palace and court is so far kept up, that the Jews often spoke of "books" in heaven in which men's deeds are recorded. Not only do we read in Slavonic Enoch 19:5 of "angels who are over the souls of men, and who write down all their works and their lives before the face of the Lord"; and in the Apocalypse of John, where symbolism abounds, of "books" being "opened" and of the "dead" being "judged according to what was written in the books"; but even in an Epistle of St. Paul we read of those "whose names are in the book of life" (Ph 4:3), and in He 12:23, of "the church of the first-born who are enrolled in heaven"; and precisely in accord with the above our Lord bade his disciples rejoice, because their names "are written down in heaven", that is, enrolled for honour (Lu 10:20).[42]

The prologue to Job shows God consulting with his royal council (Jb 1:6-12 and 2:1-6). The poet paints a spectacular scene of God doing as kings do: holding receptions and audiences on certain days. The *"sons of God"* are the supernatural courtiers who throng the palace, and who comprise the King's royal advisers. For a similar picture see 1 Kg 22:19-22; Is 6:8.

Notice though the psalmist's boldness. These mighty nobles may be paragons of beauty, wisdom, and strength, but still he exhorts them never to forget that their splendour fades before the majesty of the King (Ps 29:1-2).

According to a variant reading of De 32:8 (" ... *when he determined the number of the sons of God"*), the rabbis reckoned that the heavenly council consisted of 72 angels, one for each nation upon the earth. The church Fathers adopted that ancient tradition -

> Every nation has an angel, to whom God has committed the government of that nation ... For the Most High God, who alone holds the power of all things, has divided all the nations of the earth into 72 parts, and over these he hath appointed angels as princes.[43]

This image of a heavenly court with its royal council was probably borrowed by Israel from her pagan neighbours. But it was drastically altered to fit Israel's stern monotheism. Hence the many "gods" of the pagans were demoted either to angels or to sons of God

---

[42]   Hastings, op. cit., pg 54.

[43]   From an anonymous work, dated c. 250, The Recognitions of Clement, Bk 2, ch 42.

C. A HEAVENLY ARMY

The depiction of angels as an awesome celestial army, and of Michael as one of the *"chief princes"* who lead the heavenly hosts, confirms the belief that the angels are arranged in a hierarchy. The very term "army" requires the ideas of organisation, military rank, command, discipline, and so on -

> *Behold, the mountain was full of horses and chariots of fire (2 Kg 6:17).*
>
> *Dominion and fear are with God ... Is there any number to his armies? (Jb 25:3).*
>
> *More than twelve legions of angels (Mt 26:53).*
>
> *And the armies of heaven, arrayed in fine linen white and pure, followed (the King of kings) on white horses (Re 19:14).*

With such a host on our side, warring on our behalf, we have little reason to fear what the enemy can do to us!

III. SERAPHIM AND CHERUBIM

A. SERAPHIM

> *I saw the Lord sitting upon a throne, high and lifted up; and his train filled the temple. Above him stood the seraphim; and each had six wings: with two he covered his face, and with two he covered his feet, and with two he flew. And one called to another and said: "Holy, holy, holy is the Lord of Hosts; the whole earth is full of his glory" ... Then flew one of the seraphim to me, having in his hand a burning coal which he had taken with tongs from the altar. And he touched my mouth, and said: "Behold, this*

*has touched your lips, your guilt is taken away, and
your sin forgiven" (Is 6:1-7).*

The word *"seraphim"* means "the fiery ones" or "the noble ones".
It occurs only in this passage, and it appears to describe a group of
angels who are the throne-guardians of God. Many commentators
believe that the six-winged seraphim represent the highest angelic
order, with the four-winged cherubim perhaps occupying a slightly
lower rank - but there is insufficient information in scripture to
make the matter certain.

As "the fiery ones" the task of the seraphim appears to be:

♦ to protect the throne of God by their blazing glory.

♦ to reveal the character of God (*"our God is a consuming
fire,"* He 12:29).

♦ by hiding their form and features, to forbid the making of
any image of deity (*"Take heed to yourselves lest you ...
make a graven image in the form of anything which the
Lord your God has forbidden you. For the Lord your God
is a devouring fire, a jealous God."* De 4:23-24).

♦ to represent the irresistible power of God (*"the Lord your
God is he who goes over before you as a devouring fire"*
De 9:3).

♦ to isolate that holy throne from all that is sinful (*" ...
trembling has seized the godless: 'Who among us can dwell
with the devouring fire? Who among us can dwell with
everlasting burnings?'"* Is 33:14).

♦ to burn up the sin that keeps men away from God (Is 6:6,7).

♦ to display the absolute transcendence of God, and his
infinite holiness, which is so great that in the presence of
the Majesty On High even these resplendent beings must
reverently cover their faces and give homage to the King.

B. CHERUBIM

I accept the widely held notion that *"the living creatures"* seen by Ezekiel and John are identical with the beings elsewhere called cherubim; I also accept, although it is not actually stated in scripture, that cherubim are a class of angels. If this is so, then they can be defined as those angels in the monarchy of heaven who are the throne-bearers of God.

The offices of throne-guardians and throne-bearers were highly esteemed in Oriental palaces, and the heavenly counterparts of these earthly courtiers appear to be respectively the seraphim and the cherubim. Scripture tells us some fascinating things about the cherubim -

1. THEIR APPEARANCE

The cherubim are more vividly described, and more often mentioned in scripture (some 90 references) than any other class of angel. Ezekiel gives a stunning description of them, and that of John is hardly less colourful - see Ez 1:4-28; 10:1-22; Re 4:5-11.

Based on such visions, it seems that the cherubim, when made visible to human eyes, usually appear as hybrid celestial beings, predominantly human, but with animal and birdlike characteristics.

Belief in cherubim, or at least in creatures like them, was widespread in ancient Near Eastern civilisations. The Egyptians and Assyrians created majestic sculptures of winged beasts, and set them in place as guardians of the royal palaces. The biblical descriptions of cherubim strikingly resemble these winged beasts. The figures carved on the walls of Solomon's temple probably did not differ greatly from those adorning the walls of temples in Babylon or Thebes. Nor did the images embroidered on the temple veil, and the statues sculpted upon the mercy seat (Ex 25:17-22; 26:32; 36:8,35; 1 Kg 6:23-29,32,35; Ez 41:18-20,25; see the illustration below.)

When seen by men and women, the cherubim took on different shapes, according to the needs of each circumstance:

- the cherubim overshadowing the ark each had two wings and one face, presumably, but not necessarily, human (Ex 25:20; 1 Kg 6:25-29).

- the cherubim seen by Ezekiel at the river Chebar each had four wings and four faces (man, lion, ox, eagle; Ez 1:6,10).

- he saw the same creatures a year later, while he was in his own house, but with some differences: the faces were now those of a cherub, man, lion, and eagle (10:14); and there seemed to be more attention placed on *"the whirling wheels"* (vs. 13), and on the number of eyes (vs. 12).

- many years later the prophet described the cherubim again, in the form in which they were to be carved upon the temple walls: they were set between palm trees, and they had only two faces, a man and a young lion (41:18-19).

- John saw them, like Ezekiel, with each having the faces of a lion, ox, man, eagle, and with a multitude of eyes, but resembling the seraphim in their possession of six wings and in their song around the throne of God (Re 4:6- 8).

2. THEIR ROLE

OT descriptions of the cherubim appear to emphasise

- their wisdom (with their many eyes they see and know all that is happening);

- their mobility (shown by their wings);

- their special function and power as the bearers of God's glorious throne (shown by the whirling wheels).

In the NT they are seen more as celestial attendants of God whose special function is to call all heaven to praise and worship the

Lord; but they also act as revealers of the purpose and judgments of the Almighty (Re 6:1; 15:7).

In more detail -

a. Exalted Guardians of the Tree of Life (Ge 3:24)

Their appointment immediately after the Fall to man's original place in the Garden, and to his office in connection with the tree of life, linked with their current place around the throne of God, is both typical and prophetical of man's destiny to be exalted to highest heaven at God's side.[44]

Notice that cherubim are first mentioned in the role of gate-keepers. This suggests their close connection with the winged beasts of Assyria and Egypt, whose primary task also was to stand as guardians at the entrances of palaces and temples.

b. Exalted Bearers of the Throne of God

He rode on a cherub, and flew; he was seen upon the wings of the wind (2 Sa 22:11; Ps 18:10).

Now the glory of the God of Israel had gone up from the cherubim on which it rested (Ez 9:3).

Then the glory of the Lord went forth ... and stood over the cherubim. And the cherubim lifted up their wings and mounted up ... and the glory of the God of Israel was over them (Ez 10:18-19; 11:22).

David drew a plan for *"the golden chariot of the cherubim that spread their wings and covered the ark of the covenant of the Lord"* (1 Ch 28:18), thus showing he saw the cherubim as the charioteers of the living God, the carriers of his royal throne.

---

[44]   I have lost the source of this quotation.

c. Exalted Protectors of the Mercy-Seat

Two golden cherubim sat upon the mercy seat (the lid covering the ark of the covenant) in both the tabernacle and the temple (Ex 25:17-20; 1 Kg 6:23-28). Israelites saw the mercy seat as the throne of God, with the cherubim holding high office as throne-bearers. They carried the glorious throne invisibly upon their wings, surrounding it with sanctity and reverence. Hence scripture often lauds God as the One who is *"enthroned above the cherubim"* (1 Sa 4:4; 2 Sa 6:2; 2 Kg 19:15; 1 Ch 13:6; Ps 80:1; 99:1; Is 37:16).

You will notice in some of these references, the expression *"enthroned above the cherubim"* has virtually become a name or title of God, a means of distinguishing him from all other deities. Notice also how this idea occasionally caused the people to come perilously close to turning the ark with its golden cherubim into an idol - as though the Lord God were confined to that one location. But the true worshippers of God always understood that the ark with its carved cherubim was only a symbol of the real scene in heaven, where the true cherubim carry the actual glorious throne of the Lord God (Ez 1:26; 10:1; Re 4:6).

d. Exalted Heralds of God

God speaks from between the cherubim-

> *There I will meet with you, and from above the mercy seat, from between the two cherubim that are upon the ark of the testimony, I will speak with you (Ex 25:22)*

> *... Moses ... heard the voice speaking to him from above the mercy seat that was upon the ark of the testimony, from between the two cherubim; and it spoke to him (Nu 7:89)*

> *... and there came a voice from above the firmament over their heads ... and I heard the voice of one speaking (Ez 1:25,28)*

... I heard what seemed to be a voice in the midst of the four living creatures (Re 6:6).

IV. MICHAEL AND GABRIEL

A. MICHAEL

You will find the word archangel (*"chief messenger"*) only in 1 Th 4:16 and Ju 9; it occurs only in the singular number with the definite article ("the archangel"); and Michael alone holds that title in scripture. Many commentators therefore conclude that Michael is probably the only archangel. He may even be the chief of the angels, perhaps ranking just below the seraphim and cherubim. The main difference between angels (including the archangel), and seraphim and cherubim, appears to be that the latter are ministers around the throne of God, whereas the former (as their name suggests) are the "messengers" of God to men.

Michael is also designated *"[one of the chief* (celestial) *princes"* in Da 10:13, which seems to weaken the argument that he is supreme among the angels. It may indicate there are other archangels who have an equal standing with Michael.

On the other hand, he is called *"one of the chief princes"* in particular connection with the suzerainty of certain angels over specific nations. In this context Michael appears to have a special task as the guardian angel of Israel -

> *There is none who contends by my side against these except Michael, your prince ... At that time shall arise Michael, the great prince who has charge of your people (Da 10:21; 12:1).*

As Israel's champion, Michael contended against the demon princes of Greece and Persia (Da 10:11-14,20-21), and perhaps the title *"one of the chief princes"* belongs to him only in that role.

Otherwise he remains leader of all the angels and the only archangel.

Michael, means "Who is like God", a fitting title for "the great prince" who especially represents the Deity on earth , while the seraphim and cherubim represent him in heaven. Perhaps Michael leads the company of angels that serve God away from the throne; while the seraphim head the company that serve God around the throne.

Michael will continue to fulfil his role as the patron of Israel and as the warrior leader of the armies of heaven until the return of Christ. In the troubled days at the end of the age, just before the resurrection, he will continue to defend the people of God (Da 12:1).

The OT picture of Michael is continued in the NT. He is the immensely powerful commander of the heavenly hosts in their conflict with the forces of evil. He is seen as the main protagonist for God against the angelic prince of evil, Satan, and he is now the militant guardian not only of Israel, but also of the church.

Apocryphal writings provided the base for the passage in Jude (vs. 9; cp. De 34:6). They taught that Satan claimed the body of Moses on the ground of his control over all material things. The devil also argued that Moses' murder of the Egyptian placed him under unholy jurisdiction. Michael disputed those claims, and rescued the body of Moses from Satan's desecration. Presumably no other angel was strong enough to contend with the devil on this (or possibly any other) matter (cp. Da 10:13).

The same picture is given in *Revelation 12:7-9* -

> *Now war arose in heaven, Michael and his angels fighting against the dragon; and the dragon and his angels fought, but they were defeated ...*

Defeated, but not destroyed. Ultimate victory over the "dragon" cannot be gained by the angels, not even when they are led by Michael. That final conquest can be wrought by Christ alone -

> *Then I saw heaven opened, and behold, a white horse! He who sat upon it is called Faithful and True, and in righteousness he judges and makes war ... On his robe and on his thigh he has a name inscribed, King of kings and Lord of lords (Re 19:11-16).*

However, the King does not fight alone. With joy he shares his strength and his victory with his holy ones. John saw Christ accompanied by *"the armies of heaven, arrayed in fine linen, white and pure, following him on white horses"* (vs. 14). Against these resplendent and awful antagonists the dragon and his armies are helpless, and they are quickly overthrown (vs. 19-21).

Possible further references to Michael are:

♦ He may be spoken of in many places in the OT that talk about an "angel of the Lord" defending or helping Israel against her foes (e.g. 2 Kg 19:35).

♦ According to Jewish tradition he was the angel who gave the law to Moses on Mt. Sinai.

♦ a particular interpretation of De 33:2 gave rise to that tradition, which was also embraced by the early Christians (Ac 7:38,53; Ga 3:19; He 2:2)

♦ Josephus records the same opinion:

♦ ... we have learned from God the most excellent of our doctrines, and the most holy part of our law, by angels or ambassadors[45] ...

---

[45]   Antiquities, Bk 15, ch 5.

- ◆ the words are Herod's, who was saying that just as ambassadors are sacrosanct when they are acting officially, so do the laws of Israel derive a sacred authority from being carried between God and man by divine messengers, the angels.

- ◆ He is probably the archangel described in 1 Th 4:16, who will herald the return of Christ.

- ◆ He is probably the angel who after the last great war in heaven will seize the defeated dragon and cast him into the bottomless pit (Re 20:1-3).

Two things deserve comment here. First, we can be grateful for the knowledge that Michael and his angels are restraining the hordes of darkness; for who can tell what horrors the powers of evil would unleash upon the earth if they were not held in check (cp. Re 7:1-3; 12:12-17). Second, when even the mightiest of the angels of God prevail over the dragon only with difficulty, how remarkable it is that the humblest believer in Christ has complete personal mastery over Satan in Jesus' name!

B. GABRIEL

"Gabriel" means "God Is Great", or some would prefer "Man of God". As one of the chief heavenly servants of God he occupies a prominent place in all three faiths, Judaism, Christianity, and Islam. Both the Bible and the Koran depict Gabriel as a special messenger of God to man.

1. IN THE OT

When Daniel saw his frightening vision of the Ram and the He-Goat (Da 8:1-27), he was greatly dismayed. But as he stood perplexed, yearning to understand what he had seen, suddenly

> *there stood before (him) one having the appearance of a man. And (he) heard a man's voice ... and it*

*called, "Gabriel, make this man understand this
vision" (vs. 15-16).*

Gabriel approached Daniel, who promptly fell on his face,
trembling with fright. In pity, the angel touched the man, and
Daniel *"fell into a deep sleep"*, during which the vision was
explained to him. It foretold the destruction of the Persian empire
by Alexander the Great (356-323 BC).

Later, the same angel gave Daniel the prophecy of the Seventy
Weeks (Da 9:20-27), which told how long the Jews would remain
oppressed, when Jerusalem would be rebuilt, and when the
Messiah would appear.

The anonymous angel who brought to Samson's barren mother the
news, *"You shall conceive and bear a son,"* (Jg 13:3) was probably
Gabriel; and it was also probably he who appeared to Daniel on the
banks of the Tigris (Da 10:4 ff.). The latter vision conveys a vivid
impression of the overwhelming majesty of the heavenly
Messenger -

> *I lifted up my eyes and looked, and behold a man
> clothed in linen, whose loins were girded with gold
> of Uphaz. His body was like beryl, his face like the
> appearance of lightning, his eyes like flaming
> torches, his arms and legs like the gleam of
> burnished bronze, and the sound of his words like
> the noise of a multitude (vs. 5-6).*

So awesome was the angelic presence, even though the men who
were with Daniel did not see the vision, still *"a great trembling fell
upon them, and they fled to hide themselves"* (vs. 7). As for Daniel,
his terrors were multiplied, and were barely lessened by the angel's
compassionate touch -

> *So I was left alone and saw this great vision, and no
> strength was left in me; my radiant appearance was
> fearfully changed, and I retained no strength ... I fell*

*on my face in a deep sleep with my face to the
ground. And behold, a hand touched me and set me
trembling on my hands and knees ... When he had
spoken to me ... I turned my face to the ground and
was dumb. And behold, one in the likeness of the
sons of men touched my lips; then I opened my
mouth and spoke. I said to him who stood before
me, "O my lord, by reason of the vision pains have
come upon me, and I retain no strength ... For now
no strength remains in me, and no breath is left in
me." Again one having the appearance of a man
touched me and strengthened me ...*

Notice how the angel, to aid the fainting prophet, abandoned the
more terrifying aspects of his appearance, and in the latter part of
the vision twice appeared to Daniel simply in the form of a man
(vs. 16,18).

2. IN THE NT

Gabriel appeared to Zechariah to announce the future pregnancy of
Elizabeth and the birth of John the Baptist (Lu 1:11-13,19). Along
with that, Gabriel identified himself as an angel *"who stands in the
presence of God"* - which is a declaration of exalted privilege. This
high rank apparently conveyed to him both authority and power to
punish Zechariah with the harsh penalty of dumbness (vs. 20-23).

Gabriel fulfilled his highest role when he was sent to Mary, to tell
her she was the one chosen to bear the Messiah, whose title is also
"Son of the Most High" (Lu 1:26-33). Her cousin Elizabeth was
then six months pregnant with John. Gabriel greeted Mary with the
famous words (in Latin), "Ave Maria" ("Hail Mary!"), and told her
that her Son would establish upon the throne of David a kingdom
that will never end. Frightened and troubled, Mary wondered how
such things could be, for she was still a virgin. Gabriel gave her
only a veiled reply, for here was a mystery of divine grace and
power, beyond telling in human words -

The Holy Spirit will come upon you,
and the power of the Most High will overshadow you;
Therefore the Child to be born will be called holy,
the Son of God (Lu 1:35).

In Matthew's version of the story, the angel, unnamed but presumably Gabriel, appears to Joseph, Mary's espoused husband, and warns him not to reject her because of her pregnancy, but to take her for his wife. Gabriel announced -

> *That which is conceived in her is of the Holy Spirit;*
> *she will bear a son, and you shall call his name*
> *Jesus, for he will save his people from their sins (Mt*
> *1:18-24).*

3. IN CHURCH TRADITION

Very early, several stories about Gabriel became part of the traditions of the church. For example, a late second century work tells how Gabriel appeared to Joachim and Anna, the traditional parents of Mary, to announce to them the coming birth of their daughter. Anna was lamenting her barren state, envying some sparrows in a nest who were feeding their young, when -

> ... behold, an angel of the Lord stood by, saying, "Anna, Anna, the Lord hath heard thy prayer, and thou shalt conceive, and bring forth; and thy seed shall be spoken of in all the world" ... (And) an angel of the Lord went down to (Joachim), saying, "Joachim, Joachim, the Lord God hath heard thy prayer. Go down hence; for behold, thy wife Anna shall conceive" ... And behold, Joachim came with his flocks; and Anna stood by the gate, and saw Joachim coming, and she ran and hung upon his neck, saying, "Now I know that the Lord God hath

blessed me exceedingly" ... And Joachim rested the first day in his house.[46]

The same source fills in the story of Gabriel's later appearance to Mary, who was at her own home, and had gone out to draw some water -

> And she took the pitcher, and went out to fill it with water. And, behold, a voice saying, "Hail, thou who hast received grace; the Lord is with thee; blessed art thou among women!" And she looked round, on the right hand and on the left, to see whence this voice came. And she went away, trembling, to her house, and put down the pitcher ... And behold, an angel of the Lord stood before her, saying, "Fear not, Mary; for thou hast found grace before the Lord of all, and thou shalt conceive, according to his word ... And she was about sixteen years old when these mysteries happened.[47]

Other ancient traditions said that Gabriel was the angel who brought the good news of the Saviour's birth to the shepherds of Bethlehem; and he was the one who strengthened Jesus in the Garden of Gethsemane, prior to his anguished prayer (Lu 2:10; 22:43-44). Gabriel, they said, also has the task of watching over childbirth, and of being, with Michael, the guardian of the church against the devil.[48]

In summary: Michael is the great warrior prince, the captain of the hosts of heaven in their war against the powers of evil, the militant protector of God's Israel, both national and spiritual. Gabriel is the

---

[46]   The Protevangelium of James, ch. 4; anonymous; from Roberts and Donaldson, op. cit., vol 8, pg. 362.

[47]   Ibid., pg. 363,364.

[48]   Metford, op. cit., Gabriel, pg. 106

interpreter of God to men, a special messenger of mercy, promise, and salvation. These take their place in the great hierarchy of angels, which together fill heaven with glory, power, majesty, holiness, and praise.

CHAPTER SIX

ANGELS AT WORK

I saw in the visions of my head as I lay in bed, and, behold, a Watcher, a Holy One, came down from heaven (Da 4:13)

As Daniel dreamed, his eyes opened to see one of the mighty governors of heaven, vigilant to do God's will, coming from the throne of God. His purpose? To impose the will of the Sovereign Lord upon Nebuchadnezzar.

Do you suppose that scene could be repeated? Of course! Because angels are still at work upon planet earth!

But what advantage is there in knowing that? Since the angels, no matter how busy, are normally unseen and unfelt, does it matter if we know they are there?

THE DISCOVERY OF YOURSELF

One of the special benefits of understanding angels is a better understanding of myself. Against the background of the angelic creation I see with a keener eye my own humanness. Indeed, I cannot think about angels without being drawn irresistibly to think more deeply about myself. More simply, when I know who the angels are I come closer to knowing who I am!

As the nature of a solid object is better understood when it is contrasted with a liquid, and as darkness is known by contrasting it with light, so a vision of the angelic realm brings into sharper focus our view of mankind and of the material realm in which we live. The more knowing you can be about the angels, the more insight you will have into your own soul.

Are your eyes open to the world of angels? Then you will feel more pungently the substance of your own human nature - its strength and its weakness, its glory and debasement, its lowliness and its splendour. You can more satisfyingly slot yourself into the great scheme of things.

Although as far as I know I have not yet seen an angel, I am grateful to God for making the image of his angels vivid in my mind and spirit.

Yet I suppose the most important aspect of the doctrine of angels is the revelation scripture gives of the manifold work done by these divine messengers.

THE SERVICE THEY RENDER

There is a common impression that angels do not fill a very significant role on earth, even if they are important in heaven. But scripture shows that the angels serve both God and man in tasks of astonishing variety and value. The implication is that their ministry is an essential part of the divine plan of the ages. Frustration will confront the purposes of God if these mighty servants do not fulfil their duties.

Of course, if he so chose, God could do without angels, just as he could do without man. But the fact remains, the Lord in his wisdom and love has decreed this: his purposes will remain thwarted if they lack the willing and devoted service of his children, both human and angelic. The angels share with us the designation *"sons of God"*, and their role in the good order and success of the kingdom of God is at least equal in importance to ours.

Are we not called to serve both God and our neighbour? So too the angels have a double function: they minister in heaven and on earth, and in each dimension they render service both to God and man.

- They serve God: *"Bless the Lord, all his hosts, his ministers that do his will"* (Ps 103:21).

- They serve man: *"Are they not all ministering spirits sent forth to serve, for the sake of those who are to obtain salvation?"* (He 1:14).

I. THE ANGELS SERVE GOD

A. THEY WORSHIP GOD IN HEAVEN

The popular image of angels as harp-pluckers, singing anthems in the skies, is not wholly wrong; in fact, it reflects what is the most noble function of the angels, their highest honour and their chief joy: they surround the throne of God and fill heaven with rapturous worship and praise.

I have already written that heaven may be thought of as a royal palace, as a council chamber, and as a military headquarters. But more than all these it should be thought of as a temple, a place of worship -

1. THE LORD IN HIS TEMPLE

The Lord in his holy temple, the Lord's throne is in heaven (Ps 11:4).

In my distress I called upon the Lord ... From his temple he heard my voice, and my cry to him reached his ears (Ps 18:6).

I saw the Lord sitting upon a throne, high and lifted up; and his train filled the temple (Is 6:1).

The Lord is in his holy temple; let all the earth keep silence before him (Ha 2:20).

(They) serve him day and night within his temple; and he who sits upon the throne will shelter them with his presence (Re 7:15; see also 11:19; 16:1).

2. THE LORD ON HIS THRONE

God has established his royal throne in the heavenly temple, and there also the angels gather to worship the eternal King. Like its earthly counterparts, this temple has

♦ an altar: Re 8:5; 9:13

♦ censers: Re 5:8; 8:3

♦ sacred scrolls: Re 5:1

♦ a sacrificial victim: Re 5:6,9

♦ a holy place and ark: Re 11:19

♦ musicians: Re 5:8 (*"each holding a harp"*); 15:2 (*"standing with harps of God in their hands"*).

♦ and worshippers praising God in song and prayer: Re 5:9; 14:3; 15:2-3.

These worshippers are *"all the angels"* (Re 7:11; He 1:6), and they number countless myriads (Re 5:11).

3. THE ANGELS IN HIS PRESENCE

Among that thronging host there are seven, called *"Angels of the Presence"*, who hold the privilege beyond all others of standing nearest to the throne, and of acting as the special servants of God (Is 63:9; Re 1:4; 5:6; 8:2).

The angel Gabriel is one of those *"who stand in the presence of God"* (Lu 1:19). The outer court cannot confine him, nor even the holy place, but he enters *"within the veil"*, into the holiest of all, and there ministers beneath the full radiance of the Lord God (cp. He 6:19-20).

The *Angels of the Presence*, perhaps the highest order of the hierarchy, offer God the most exalted and holy praise. That is their peculiar prerogative. But the remainder of the heavenly host are by no means excluded from the joy of worship. There is not one of them who would claim any greater happiness than to obey the injunction, *"Praise him, all his angels, praise him, all his host!"* (Ps 148:2). With glad acclamations they all come from time to time to stand with the holy assembly and to anthem the glory of God.

4. THE PRAISE OF HIS GLORY

The angels worship the Father, and they worship the Son. How joyfully they share the rapture we know when we worship Christ. Scripture declares that all of the angels delight to honour the Son, and to surround him with praise: *"When he brings the first-born into the world, he says, 'Let all God's angels worship him!'"* (He 1:6).

5. THE SHARERS OF HIS GRACE

Just as we come joyfully into the place of worship, and stand at the table of Christ, filled with adoration, praise, and thanksgiving, so the angels behold his wounds in heaven, and seek every opportunity to mingle their songs with the prayers of the saints. They worship him in admiration of the redemption he has accomplished for man; and they worship him because their own destiny is inextricably woven into that of the church.

The victory Christ has gained for the church is also their victory. The glorification of the church will bring glory to those who have ministered to the church. The witness of his wounds in heaven, when he stands among them like a Lamb that has been slain, has a meaning for them as deep and wonderful as it has for us, although in a different manner. They have as much cause to adore him as we have, for did he not keep them out of the kingdom of darkness, and has he not given them a place of magnificence in the coming kingdom of God?

It is not surprising then, when John saw a vision of all the angels gathered in heaven for worship, he saw them standing around the throne of Christ, joining their praises with those of the church -

> *I saw a Lamb standing, as though it had been slain ... and the twenty-four elders fell down before the Lamb, each holding a harp, and with golden bowls full of incense, which are the prayers of the saints ... and I heard around the throne ... the voice of many angels, numbering myriads of myriads and thousands of thousands, saying with a loud voice, "Worthy is the Lamb who was slain, to receive power and wealth and wisdom and might and honour and glory and blessing!" And I heard every creature in heaven and on earth and under the earth and in the sea, and all therein, saying, "To him who sits upon the throne and to the Lamb be blessing and honour and glory and might for ever and ever! (Re 5:6-14).*

B. THEY REJOICE IN GOD'S CREATION

> *Where were you when I laid the foundation of the earth ... when the morning stars sang together, and all the sons of God shouted for joy? (Jb 38:4-7).*

The poet talks about angels rejoicing in God's natural works. They observe the wonders of creation with limitless admiration. With amazement they behold the handiwork of God. They see the infinite wisdom and power of God displayed in earth, sky, ocean, and in all that dwells in them, and they are glad.

The psalmist knew it was part of the duty of the angels to praise God for the marvels of the universe. So he prefaced his stirring poem about the majesty of a thunderstorm with a rousing injunction to the angels to praise God for this most awesome display of natural power -

Ascribe to the Lord, O heavenly beings, ascribe to the Lord glory and strength. Ascribe to the Lord the glory of his name; worship the Lord in holy array (29:1).

C. THEY DO THE WILL OF GOD

Eventually the will of God is done by every creature. It is impossible for his will to be ultimately thwarted. *"He does whatever he pleases, in heaven and on earth!"* (Ps 135:6). The fallen angels and the unfallen alike do the will of God: they can do nothing at all unless he permits it; and all their behaviour results in the full accomplishment of God's purpose. No part of the Almighty's plan can fail. All that has ever happened, or ever will happen, whether in heaven, on earth, or in hell, will finally coalesce into the perfect consummation of the Father's unwavering resolve.

Yet although the kingdom of darkness serves the purpose of God as surely as the kingdom of heaven, there remains a vast gulf between them. For there are two ways to do the will of God: by coercion, or by choice. The denizens of darkness serve God, yielding to his command, because they must. They fear his power; they tremble before his might. But the holy angels serve God because they love him. It is their pleasure to do his will. Their service is wholly voluntary. They are happily obedient sons, not reluctantly driven slaves.

The angels do not serve God mindlessly; they are not dispassionate robots; their obedience is not mere reflex, like the conditioned response of an animal to the command of its trainer. They serve God as free moral agents, with a capacity to determine the manner of their service, and with a power of choice in the methods they employ. Their service is an expression of dynamic holiness, not of dread compulsion. They think, they plan, they act to do the will of

God in whatever way is best suited to their personal wisdom, skill, and strength.

That is why the psalmist, when he spoke of the pure obedience of the angels, was able to recognise in them a compliance similar to his own; for just as he bade his own soul to bless the Lord, so likewise he bade the angels -

> *Bless the Lord, O you his angels, you mighty ones who do his work, hearkening to the voice of his word! Bless the Lord, all his hosts, his ministers that do his will! Bless the Lord, all his works, in all places of his dominion. Bless the Lord, O my soul! (Ps 103: 20-21).*

D. THEY EXECUTE THE JUDGMENTS OF GOD

> Angels assist in God's judgment. Enough instances are on record to show that this is continually being done in human history ... A striking example of this is the death of Herod Agrippa: *"Immediately an angel of the Lord smote him, because he did not give God the glory; and he was eaten by worms and died"* (Ac 12:23). Some examples of their roles in judgment are shown in the visions of John on Patmos. One angel with great authority and amazing splendour proclaimed the fall of Rome (Re 18:1-12). In the outset of the war in which Christ and his heavenly armies defeated the beast and his cohorts, an angel stood in the sun and summoned carrion fowl to eat the corpses of God's enemies to be slain in the conflict (19:17 f).[49]

---

[49] Pictorial Encyclopedia of the Bible, Vol One; article *Angel*, pg. 166. Zondervan Publishing House, Grand Rapids, Michigan. 1975. Remember also Lord Byron's poem, which I have cited on pg. 31 above.

1. A TERRIBLE COMMISSION

At the time of the exodus, an angel of the Lord passed through the land of Egypt, killing the first-born of every man and beast unprotected by the blood of the covenant (Ex 12:23). Seventy thousand people died in Israel, when an angel stretched out his hand over the land and ravaged it with pestilence (2 Sa 24:15-16). In one night a terrible plague unleashed by an angel of God annihilated an Assyrian army (2 Kg 19:35). So appalling was that display of angelic power, the Israelites celebrated it for centuries -

> (Sennacherib) lifted his hand against Zion
> and boasted loudly in his arrogance.
> Then their hearts and hands trembled,
> they felt the pangs of a woman in labour;
> But they called on the merciful Lord,
> stretching out their hands towards him.
> Swiftly the Holy One heard them from heaven
> and delivered them by the agency of Isaiah;
> He struck the camp of the Assyrians,
> and his Angel annihilated them *(Sir 48:18-21, NJB)*

The psalmist knew the same fear, and understood the dread power of the heavenly host, when he wrote:

> *Let them be like chaff before the wind, with the angel of the Lord driving them on! Let their way be dark and slippery, with the angel of the Lord pursuing them! (35:5-6). And John heard a loud voice from the temple telling the seven angels, "Go and pour out on the earth the seven bowls of the wrath of God" (Re 16:1).*

What a terrible commission - to *"pour out on the earth the wrath of God!"* And how relentlessly the task was done, so that the whole earth groaned in the misery of divine judgment (vs. 2-21). God commanded the seven angels and without question they obeyed.

No man, no nation, could withstand or prevent the outpoured judgment. With awful inevitability the hour must come when *"the seventh angel poured his bowl into the air, and a great voice came out of the temple, from the throne, saying, 'It is done!'"*

Who can delay those majestic servants of the Lord God? Who can hinder them from demonstrating the fury of God? With frightful violence they hasten to do the divine command. The whole earth crumbles before their will.

Do the angels take pleasure in such dreadful work?

Hardly!

Surely such dire infliction of punishment is not their natural labour, but (as it is to God) a *"strange"* work, one that is alien to their desire (cp. Is 28:21). We may say of them (as of God), they do not *"willingly afflict or grieve the sons of men"*, and they find no *"pleasure in the death of the wicked"* (La 3:33; Ez 18:23,32; 33:11). But when God has decreed destruction, they cannot do otherwise, and they become efficient and irresistible agents of his doom.

2. A PRESENT REALITY

Scripture shows the angels just as active today as they were in Bible days, inflicting the judgments of God on nations, cities, families, and individuals. However, without a divine revelation to that effect, it is impossible to tell if a particular tragedy is an act of judgment. Furthermore, it is probably perilous to delve closely into whether angelic activity lies behind any event. God may himself choose occasionally to reveal the deeper significance of what is happening; but I doubt if it is wise to ask for such a disclosure. The result of an inquiry pursued too earnestly is more likely to be demonic deception than divine revelation.

The emphasis in the NT is not upon judgment, but upon salvation, not upon sight, but upon faith. Are you a believer? Then the Father calls you to implicit trust in his providence, and to confidence that *"he is working in all things for good with those who love him, who are called according to his purpose"* (Ro 8:28). That is an affirmation of faith, dependent upon neither sight nor insight. Whether or not you understand what is happening, you can believe the outcome will be good in the Father's love.

We may deduce from the dealings of God among nations in Bible days that he deals with the nations of our world in the same way - but unlike the prophets of old, we are not usually given specific intelligence of such divine activity. Contemporary Christians who have tried to take on an OT prophetic role, and to pronounce the judgments of God on modern nations and cities, have more often been wrong than they have been right.

I cannot recall meeting even one such "prophet" who has been right. Over the past quarter-century I have read many books, articles, sermons, by people who have tried to assume the mantle of an OT prophet. So far, their predictions have failed to materialise. It seems the Holy Spirit is no longer communicating prophecies of national destruction such as he gave to the prophets of Israel. The message of the Spirit today is overwhelmingly directed to the church (not the nations) - a message of judgment beginning in the house of God, and of revival springing out of a cleansed and renewed people. However, you may take that as personal opinion, not necessarily as scriptural fact. I cannot deny that the Holy Spirit may choose at any time to give revelation to the church on any matter at all (cp. Ac 11:27-30).

I believe, then, that angels, as agents of divine judgment, are as active today as they were in Bible days. But I am unwilling to specify any single event as an act of judgment, and I remain *suspicious* of any attempt to do so.

A more important aspect of the work of angels in judgment will take place in the future, when Christ returns -

E. THEY WILL ATTEND CHRIST ON THE LAST DAY

1. THE ANGELS WILL BE HIDDEN NO LONGER

Just as we are now working continually for God, but awaiting the real consummation of our hope and love at the resurrection on the day of Christ's return, so the angels share a similar hope. Although they are fully employed now in the service of God, the second advent will apparently be as much a day of consummation for them as it will be for the church. That day will disclose all the sons of God, whether angelic or earthly.

For the moment our real identity is as much hidden from the world as theirs is; but on that day the whole earth will see the manifestation of all the sons of God (Ro 8:19-21). For us: the clay will fall from our frame and God will transform us into the radiant image of Christ, blazing with a glory outshining the sun. For the angels: the veil will be torn away from the spirit world, and the vast heavenly host will become visible to the astonished nations, who will gaze in wonder at the glittering legions. As scripture says-

a. It will be a Day of Revelation of the Saints

I consider that the sufferings of the present time are not worth comparing with the glory that is to be revealed to us. For the creation waits with eager longing for the revealing of the sons of God ... because the creation itself will be set free from its bondage to decay and obtain the glorious liberty of the children of God (Ro 8:18-21) ... (God will) grant rest with us to you who are afflicted, when the Lord Jesus is revealed from heaven with his mighty angels in flaming fire ... when he comes on that day to be glorified in his saints, and to be marvelled at in all who have believed (2 Th 1:7-10).

b. It will be a Day of Revelation of the Angels

The Son of man is to come with his angels in the glory of his Father, and then he will repay every man for what he has done (Mt 16:27) ... When the Son of man comes in his glory, and all the angels with him, then he will sit on his glorious throne (25:31).

Like us, the angels are waiting for the day of Christ's return to bring them to their full honour. Until that day comes, they remain, like us, to some extent unfulfilled, their potential unrealised. But then they will blaze in all the splendour of their supernal glory, and rejoice in the attainment of their true purpose. Hidden and constrained no longer, nor compelled to work behind a veil, they will share joyfully with the saints the endlessly increasing prosperity of the kingdom of God.

2. THEY WILL GATHER THE SAINTS TOGETHER

The first task of the angels on the day of Christ's return, will be to call the saints forth from their graves, to catch up the living believers, and to gather the entire raptured church into the presence of the Lord. It is impossible to conceive the brilliance of this event, nor the immensity of the power God will unleash through the angels when the church is caught up to meet her King!

> At the round earth's imagined corners, blow
>   Your trumpets, angels, and arise, arise
> From death, you numberless infinities
>   Of souls, and to your scattered bodies go,
> All whom the flood did, and fire shall o'erthrow,
>   All whom war, dearth, age, agues, tyrannies,
> Despair, law, chance, hath slain, and you whose eyes

Shall behold God, and never taste death's woe![50]

So the arousing sound of the archangel's voice will shatter the silent skies; the dead will rise from their graves, and together with the living believers, rise to meet the coming Christ (1 Th 4:16).

However, Paul does not ascribe to the archangel unaided power to raise the dead - for an irresistible *"cry of command"* from the descending Lord himself must precede the archangel's shout, and the dread clarion of *"the trumpet of God"* alone can consummate the resurrection. Victory over death belongs uniquely to Christ, but he is able to communicate that victory to any of his servants. His gift of life is what will make the cry of the archangel so efficacious.

Jesus himself said that -

> *He will send out his angels with a loud trumpet call,*
> *and they will gather his elect from the four winds,*
> *from one end of heaven to the other (Mt 24:31).*

Paul, with a nice touch, draws no distinction between the heavenly and earthly children of God. He says that the unfallen angels and redeemed man will alike share in the glory of Christ's return. He calls them all *"saints"* -

> *May the Lord establish your hearts unblameable in*
> *holiness before our God and Father, at the coming*
> *of our Lord Jesus with all his saints (1 Th 3:13).*

---

[50] Holy Sonnets, John Donne, first printed in 1633. The opening lines refer to Re 7:1, and the sonnet describes the re-uniting in the resurrection of souls with their bodies, which have been "scattered" among the dust of the earth. Some were destroyed in the ancient Flood, some will be destroyed in the Fire of the Last Day, others perished through a variety of natural calamities, and there are some who will not die, but will be alive on earth when the Lord comes ("you whose eyes shall behold God"). But all will be called up and called together by the sounding trumpets of the angels.

3. THEY WILL POUR OUT THE WRATH OF GOD

The work of judgment done by the angels across the centuries of human history will find its awful denouement in one final outburst of divine fury -

> *Behold, the Lord is coming with his holy myriads, to*
> *execute judgment on all, and to convict the ungodly*
> *of all their deeds of ungodliness which they have*
> *committed in such an ungodly way, and of all the*
> *harsh things which ungodly sinners have spoken*
> *against him (Jude 14-15).*

Those words were spoken by Enoch, who lived far back in history, only the seventh generation from Adam. How long the angels have waited! What evils they have seen upon the earth! How many times they have yearned to support the godly and smash the ungodly! But the wisdom and command of God restrained them.

Yet they know the word of God cannot be broken. They wait the day of vengeance. How terrible the recompense then meted upon the enemies of God, and how munificent the rewards heaped upon his true servants!

Paul caught a glimpse of that same awful day, a day of fiery doom, a day of outpoured wrath, a day of punishment and of eternal destruction -

> *The Lord Jesus will be revealed from heaven with*
> *his mighty angels in flaming fire, inflicting*
> *vengeance upon those who do not know God and*
> *upon those who do not obey the gospel of our Lord*
> *Jesus Christ (2 Th 1:7-9).*

But the most terrible vision of all was seen by John on Patmos: the vision of the Angel of the Sickle, and of the Angel of Power Over Fire. The sharp sickle will swing! The fire will blaze! The vintage of the earth is gathered! It is thrown into the great wine press of the wrath of God! The ungodly are consumed! The judgment is completed! (Re 14:19-20).

4. THEY WILL BE WITNESSES OF THE BOOK OF LIFE

Christ emphasised the honour of having your name commended by him in the presence of the holy angels -

> *I tell you, everyone who acknowledges me before men, the Son of man also will acknowledge before the angels of God; but he who denies me before men will be denied before the angels of God (Lu 12:8-9; see also 9:26; Mk 8:38).*

And what he spoke on earth, the Lord confirmed when he spoke from heaven -

> *He who conquers shall be clad thus in white garments, and I will not blot his name out of the book of life; I will confess his name before my Father and before his angels. He who has an ear, let him hear what the Spirit says to the churches (Rev 3:5-6).*

It is as though God requires the angels to act as witnesses of the entry of each saint into the book of life. The celestial jury will confirm that God acted with impartial and perfect justice when he gave redemption to these but condemned the ungodly. Perhaps also the Judge names each saint so that "the holy angels may serve this future prince, and the evil ones may know who it is that has been wrested from their control" (J. E. Van den Brink).

5. THEY WILL PURGE THE KINGDOM

> *Just as the weeds are gathered and burned with fire, so will it be at the close of the age. The Son of man will send his angels, and they will gather out of his*

kingdom all causes of sin and all evildoers, and throw them into the furnace of fire; there many will weep and gnash their teeth. Then the righteous will shine like the sun in the kingdom of their father. He who has ears, let him hear (Mt 13:40-43).

F. CHRIST IS THEIR LINK BETWEEN HEAVEN AND EARTH

When Jesus saw Nathanael coming toward him, he said, *"Behold, an Israelite indeed, in whom is no guile!"* (Jn 1:47). The statement was full of irony, for the first Israelite, Jacob, was quite the opposite - cunning and wily. But how marvellously the grace of God has wrought! A true descendent of Jacob, a proper Israelite, is no longer renowned for craftiness, but for artless integrity and godly candour!

Thinking about Jacob reminded Christ of the strange dream the patriarch had one night near Haran -

> *Taking one of the stones of the place, he put it under his head and lay down in that place to sleep. And he dreamed that there was a ladder set up on the earth, and the top of it reached to heaven; and behold, the angels of God were ascending and descending on it! And behold, the Lord stood above it (Ge 28:11-13).*

Remembering this incident, Jesus said to Nathanael: "Truly, truly, I say to you, you will see heaven opened, and the angels of God ascending and descending upon the Son of man" (Jn 1:51).

What was Jacob's ladder, that bridge between heaven and earth, that stairway for the angels? It was none other than Christ himself! By him the angels have access to God's heaven; by him they traverse the gulf between the spiritual and material worlds; by him they have power to serve God and man. For them he is "The Way" as surely as he is for us. Without him, they, like us, can do nothing.

They ascend upon him; they descend upon him. As he is for us, so he is for them the Source of their strength, the Fount of their wisdom, the Origin of their holiness, the Centre of their praise, and the Focus of their destiny.

So for each one of the holy angels, Christ is the centre of the universe. He is all their sustenance. They serve him with joy. They worship him with song. Through him they give glory to the Lord God, their Father and ours.

II. THE ANGELS SERVE MEN AND WOMEN

By three powerful statements (He 1:6,7,13-14) the apostle tells us -

♦ that Christ is the centre of the angel's world

When he brings the First-born into the world, he says, "Let all God's angels worship him" (He 1:6).

I know I have mentioned this idea several times already; but it is important (even if this study is about angels) to keep our gaze, our admiration, our faith directed towards Christ. As great and splendid as angels may be, Christ is incomparably more worthy -

(He is) as much superior to angels as the name he has obtained is more excellent than theirs. For to what angel did God ever say, "Thou art my Son, today I have begotten thee?" Or again, "I will be to him a Father, and he shall be to me a son?" (vs 4,5; Ps 2:7; 2 Sa 7:14).

♦ the true nature and substance of the angels

Of the angels he says, "Who makes his angels winds, and his servants flames of fire" (vs 7; Ps 104:4).

Here is information as to the nature of the angelic substance. It is subtle, pervasive, mobile, energetic as wind; it is intense, brilliant, powerful as fire, and can be as destructive, when angels are employed as agents of the divine wrath. (G. H. Lang).

So the angels may be thought of as disembodied spirits of fiery essence (Michael). As mobile as the wind, as furious as devouring flames. All else that scripture says of them is more in the form of imagery, analogue, symbolism, than of literal description.

♦ the work they are sent to do -

To what angel has he ever said, "Sit at my right hand, till I make thine enemies a stool for thy feet"? Are they not all ministering spirits sent forth to serve, for the sake of those who are to obtain salvation? (vs. 13,14).

The angels are spirits; they are ministering spirits; they are sent forth to serve.

The very name angel, by which we identify these spirits, suggests their public office as the servants of God to man.

The English language (like most modern languages) uses the noun angel in a substantive sense, to define the nature of the heavenly messengers - it conjures up an image of a particular kind of supernatural spirit being. It describes for us not so much what angels do as what they are. But in the Bible the word angel says almost nothing about the nature of these beings, but almost everything about their work. Angel means messenger or servant. In particular they are messengers who serve God by helping the church. They are ministers of God to his covenant people.

It is our pleasant task now to examine this good work of the angels-

A. THEY SHARE OUR SALVATION

The destiny of the angels is irrevocably linked to that of the church; therefore they watch with intense interest and a sense of personal involvement, the unfolding drama of our redemption.

A very early hymn, quoted by Paul, shows how the first Christians understood the intertwining of angelic destiny with our salvation -

> *He was manifested in the flesh,*
> *He was vindicated in the Spirit,*
> *He was seen by angels ... (1 Ti 3:16).*

"He was seen by angels" - that is a rather mysterious statement, and commentators are not sure what the ancient song-writer meant by it. But he was at least saying that nothing in the birth, life, death, resurrection, and ascension of Christ remained unobserved by the angels. They gazed earnestly on all that Jesus did. They were witnesses of his words and works. They watched with approval, they looked with admiration, they observed with joy.

He was seen in heaven by the angels before his incarnation. He was seen on earth by the angels as he entered into victorious combat with the powers of darkness. He was again seen in heaven by the angels when he returned in triumph, leading captivity captive.

The watching angels are thus able to confirm to every creature that he who was born in Bethlehem is the eternal Lord of heaven. There is no possibility of deception, nor of mistaken identity. The heavenly witnesses will attest for ever that it was the same Christ who rose from the dead, who is now sitting at the Father's right hand, and whose everlasting right it is to reign as King of kings and Lord of lords.

Now they stand around his throne, still beholding him, and lauding him, for they know that the glory he obtained for the church will add marvellous lustre to their own destiny.

Hence, the angels were not merely the bringers of a message of joy to man (Lu 2:10-11), they participate themselves in this joy as they observe the growth of the church (15:10). The terminology used in the latter reference is unusual: there is joy before the angels of God over one sinner who repents. The idea seems to be that the angels are very glad to see the prosperity of the church, not only because they rejoice with those who are being saved, nor even because they rejoice in the Father's joy, but because the triumph of the church places before them the certainty of a future felicity beyond anything they now know.

Paul goes even further. He suggests that apart from the church the angelic creation will remain unable to accomplish the full purpose of God. The ultimate happiness of the heavenly host is inextricably dependent upon that of the church - Ep 3:9-11. The failure of the church would mean their ruin (and indeed, of the entire kingdom of God); the triumph of the church is the guarantee of their unfailing felicity.

No wonder, then, even the mightiest of the celestial princes long to look into the things that pertain to our salvation! How could they not be eager to give the heirs of salvation every help commanded or permitted by God!

B. GUARDIAN ANGELS

From ancient times people have widely accepted the notion of guardian angels; that is, the belief that each of us has a special angel on permanent assignment as our personal defender.

Is that true?

1. ORIGIN OF THE IDEA

The idea of guardian angels appeared early in Israel's history (Ge 24:7), but it remained largely undeveloped until after the Jews had returned from their exile (that is, after 538 BC). Two major influences seem to have influenced this development: the angelology of the Persians, whose culture was now dominant in the region; and an increased emphasis on the transcendence of God (brought on by the fall of Jerusalem and the Babylonian captivity).

For the Jewish people, the downfall of their capital was so catastrophic, the razing of their temple so appalling, and their bondage in a foreign land so hateful, Yahweh their God became an object of terror. Who could bear such awful holiness? Who could approach such relentless majesty? How could mortal man dare to stand in the presence of such crushing power?

So priest and worshipper alike became increasingly wary of expecting any direct communication with Yahweh. They preferred to believe that angelic mediation between man and God was essential. They wanted to distance themselves from the grim throne of the Almighty. Angels were a comforting barrier between the people and this God who had so ruthlessly broken their forefathers.

Everyone therefore welcomed angels as intervening messengers between heaven and earth. They did the work of God among men. They conveyed the prayers of the people to God. No one had to face God directly. Even Moses, it was said, received the law, not from the hand of fierce Yahweh, but rather from angelic ambassadors - an idea the apostles apparently accepted; Ac 7:38; Ga 3:19; He 2:2.[51]

---

[51] The Hebrew text of the OT makes no mention of angels giving the law to Moses; but the Greek text, translated c. 200 BC, long after the return from the exile, does add angels to the story: "The Lord has come from Sinai, and appeared from Seir to us, and has come with haste from Mount Paran with the ten thousands of his holy ones; on his right hand were his angels with him ... and he received of his words the law which Moses charged us" (De 33:2-3, LXX).

Josephus (c. 70 AD), in his Antiquities of the Jews, referred to the same tradition of angelic intervention in the giving of the law: " ... we have learned from God the most excellent of our doctrines, and the most holy part of our law, (which came) by angels, or ambassadors ... " (15.5.3).

Still later, at least among Jews who had a mystical disposition, a series of seven halls were visualised between the worshipper and the throne of God. An angel guarded the entrance to each hall, who would not allow anyone through who did not know the correct mystical password. Each talisman was made up of special combinations of letters from the Hebrew alphabet. Select initiates alone had access to the holy codes, so ordinary people were effectively insulated from God's majesty.[52]

Islam went even further, positing the existence of a separate inferior order of spirit-beings, standing between mankind and the angels. These were the jinn (English, genies), made famous by the Arabian stories of Aladdin, and the like. King Solomon was thought to have commanded cohorts of jinn when he built the Temple.[53] They could be brought under human control by the use of magic words. They too served the purpose of putting a distance between man and God. Humans who needed divine help could call upon a genie rather than risk approaching the dreadful throne of the Almighty.

Once the angels were established as intermediaries between God and man, it was easy to adopt the Persian notion that every human being has a personal patron spirit. Zoroaster himself (the Persian prophet, c. 1000 BC) apparently did not clearly teach the existence of such guardian angels. But after his death a body of doctrine developed that greatly enlarged his simple original ideas. Thus the

---

Likewise, from the anonymnus Jubilees (c. 140 BC): "And (God) said to the angel of the presence, 'Write for Moses from the first creation until my sanctuary is built in their midst' ... And the angel of the presence, who went before the camp of Israel, took the tables of the division of years from the time of the creation of the law and testimony ... And the angel of the presence spoke to Moses by the word of the Lord ... " (1:27,29; 2:1).

[52]   See Facts On File Dictionary Of Religions; ed. John R. Hinnels; Facts On File Inc, New York; 1984; pg 210, article *Merkabah Mysticism*.

[53]   Ibid., pg 174, article *Jinn*

notion became established of specific angelic protectors (called *fravashi*), assigned to accompany the devout wherever they went, and to provide individual guidance and care. No one can be sure today how much Jewish teachings were influenced by Zoroastrian doctrine, but it seems inescapable that there was some influence. Some of the rabbis went even further, arguing that God has assigned to each person two warrior angels: one to stand on the right hand, and one on the left.[54]

The early Christians adopted and expanded those Persian and Jewish ideas. For example, The Shepherd of Hermas (a second century book accepted as scripture by some ancient churches) taught that the two angels (the one on the left and the one on the right) are not the same: only one is good, the other is evil. These two accompany their ward every moment of the day, the one enticing to vice, the other to virtue. That tradition is still alive in the popular mythology of our own day; except modern tale-tellers have changed the image into a demon sitting and whispering upon one shoulder, and an angel (or conscience) on the other.

By the time of Christ many people thought that a person's guardian angel must bear a close resemblance to him - a kind of immortal clone of the mortal man. Several early Christian writings present this view, and a reflection of it can be seen in Ac 12:14-15. Rhoda exclaimed that Peter had escaped from prison and was standing at the door. The others scoffed, "You're out of your mind. It must be his angel!" They were convinced she had mistaken Peter's angelic twin for the apostle. Since the man and his angel looked alike, it was easy to confuse them.

Still later, Islam adopted the common Christian angelology of the 7th century, and it became part of the Koran -

---

[54]   Dictionary of Philosophy and Religion, ed. W. L. Reeses; Humanities Press, NJ, 1980; pg. 644.

Praise belongs to God, Creator of the heavens and the earth, who appointed angels to be his messengers, some having two, three, or four pairs of wings ... Behold, there are two Guardian Angels appointed to watch each man's deeds, to learn them and to note them. One sits on his right hand and the other on his left. For every word he utters there is a sentinel standing beside him, ready to note it ... God is (the righteous man's) Protector, and Gabriel, then good men from among the faithful, and after that, the angels will be his supporters ... Truly, angels have been appointed over you to protect you; they are noble yet kind, writing down your deeds, knowing and understanding all that you do ... Every soul has a guardian (angel) set over it; so let each man now think from what he is created.[55]

2. GUARDIAN ANGELS IN THE OT

The Persians were not the sole originators of the concept of guardian angels. The belief was an ancient one, held in one form or another by various cultures. But, by assigning a particular angel to each person, the Persians did give to the doctrine a warmly intimate form. By contrast, at least before the exile, the Hebrews preferred to think in more general terms. They knew that God did

---

[55] I have paraphrased those passages from several different translations of *Suras 35:1; 50:17-18; 66:4; 82:10-12; 86:4-5*. The number of wings signifies rank in the hierarchy, rather than a specific count. For example, George Sale writes that "Gabriel is said to have appeared to Mohammed on the night he made his journey to heaven, with no less than 600 wings." He also says, "The Mohammedans have a tradition that the angel who notes a man's good actions has the command over him who notes his evil actions; and that when a man does a good action, the angel of the right hand writes it down ten times, and when he commits an ill action, the same angel says to the angel of the left hand, 'Forbear setting it down for seven hours; peradventure he may pray, or may ask pardon.'" (The Koran, a reprint of Sales' 18th century translation; pub. by Frederick Warne, London; no date; pg. 426, 501.)

send angels to guide and care for his people, but they gave no thought to specific personal guardians. The Lord might dispatch any angel, or many, to do his will on earth, but no one expected a permanent chaperone.

Nonetheless, the prophets clearly understood that angels are protectors of the servants of God. They are heavenly paladins, spiritual knights errant, championing the rights of the Father's defenceless children. This broader vision of guardian angels can be seen in Ge 24:7; Ex 23:20-23; Nu 20:16; etc.

There is one sense, however, in which the prophets may have come near to thinking about certain angels having a particular custodial role. There are suggestions in the OT, not of personal but of national guardian angels. Citizens may not have had a permanent defender, but the prophets hint that each nation had its own heavenly prince -

> *When the Most High gave each nation its heritage,*
> *when he partitioned the human race,*
> *he assigned the boundaries of the nations*
> *according to the number of the sons of God.*

That is from the Greek text of De 32:8. The *"sons of God"* are the members of the celestial court, each of them appointed governor of a nation on earth.

Da 10:13 expresses a similar idea, except that now the governing prince is a demonic spirit, ruling over a nation hostile to Israel. In Daniel's vision, an angel explains to him why his prayer had been delayed -

> *The Prince of the kingdom of Persia resisted me for*
> *three weeks; but then Michael, one of the Chief*
> *Princes, came to help me.*

And Sir 17:17 says -

> God has appointed a ruling (angel) for every nation,

But God has reserved Israel as his own portion

♦ that is, God himself, not an angel, will be their governor.

But by the time the story of Tobit was written, the people were quite ready to accept the idea of God appointing a particular angel to guard one man -

> Tobias went out to find a man who knew the way and would accompany him to Media, and found himself face to face with the angel Raphael. Not knowing he was an angel of God, he questioned him: "Where do you come from, young man?" "I am an Israelite," he replied, "one of your fellow-countrymen, and I have come here to find work" (5:4-5; NEB).

As you will see in the next chapter, that idea was taken up by the early church and became very popular among the first Christians. But is it biblical? That also must wait for the next chapter. But let me close this one with a fine passage from the Koran, which urges all pious people to believe in angels. It is based on biblical teaching, and commands the Islamic faithful to honour the Hebrew prophets, Jesus, and the apostles -

> And We (God) gave to Moses the Book, and after him sent succeeding Messengers; and We gave Jesus son of Mary the clear signs, and confirmed him with the Holy Spirit ...

> True piety is this: to believe in God, and the Last Day,
> the angels, the Book, and the Prophets,
> to give of one's substance, however cherished,
> to kinsmen and orphans,
> the needy, the traveller, beggars,
> and to ransom the slave,

to perform the prayer, to pay the alms.
And they who fulfil their covenant
when they have engaged in a covenant,
and endure with fortitude
misfortune, hardship, and peril,
these are they who are true in their faith,
these are the truly godfearing.[56]

[56] The Koran Interpreted, *Sura 2:81,173*, tr. Arthur J Arberry; Oxford University Press, Oxford, UK.; 1964; pg. 11,23. The reference to the *Book* almost certainly means, or at least includes, the Bible. Covenant means any kind of contractual obligation

CHAPTER SEVEN

HOW THE ANGELS HELP US

"Do I really have a personal guardian angel?"

We began to explore the answer to that question in the previous chapter. So far we have looked at some general background material, the teaching of the OT, the influence of Persia, the Koran, and some early Christian ideas.

Before looking more closely at what the Bible says, here are some of the ideas about guardian angels that were popular during the first few centuries -

I. MORE ON GUARDIAN ANGELS

A. THE EARLY CHURCH

1. GENERAL REFERENCES

Thaumaturgus (whose name means Miracle Worker) was bishop of Neo-Caesarea in the middle third century. His ministry was remarkably successful. People said there were only 17 Christians when he began, and only 17 pagans when he died! The list of his miracles is formidable and astonishing.[57]

---

[57] For example, a footnote in the Ante-Nicene Fathers, Vol 6, pg 6, says: "He could move the largest stones by a word; he could heal the sick; the demons were subject to him, and were exorcised by his fiat; he could give bounds to overflowing rivers; he could dry up mighty lakes; he could cast his cloak over a man and cause his death. Once, spending a night in a heathen temple, he banished its divinities by his simple presence, and by merely placing on the altar a piece of paper bearing the words, *Gregory to Satan - enter*, he could bring the presiding demons back to their shrine ... Such were the wonders believed to signalise the life of Gregory." (Eerdman's 1978 reprint of the original set edited by Roberts and Donaldson.)

He said this about guardian angels -

> If I may seek to speak about ... any of those invisible beings ... who have a special care for men, I will speak about that being, who, by some momentous decision, had me allotted to him from my boyhood to rule, and rear, and train - I mean that holy Angel of God who fed me from my youth ... So in addition to the worship we offer to the Common Ruler of all men, we also acknowledge and praise the being, whoever he is, who has been the wonderful guide of our childhood, who in all other matters has been in time past my beneficent tutor and guardian ... that angel, I say, who still at this present time sustains, and instructs, and conducts me.[58]

Theodotus was a second-century tanner from Byzantium, who gained some renown as the leader of a short-lived sect. He believed that a guardian angel would gather infants forsaken or exposed by their parents. God made the angel responsible to rear and train the children in a secret place. When they were grown they would one day become the judges of those who had sought to kill them. The custodian chosen for this nurturing task was the angel who had presided over the conception of each child in the womb.

Clement of Alexandria was the greatest of the late second- century teachers. His ideas were so deeply planted in the church they still shape our thinking. On guardian angels he declared -

> The thoughts of virtuous men are produced through the inspiration of God ... The divine will is conveyed to human souls (by) particular divine ministers contributing to such services. For regiments of angels are distributed over the nations

---

[58]   Oration to Origen, ch 4.

and cities. And, perchance, some are assigned to individuals.[59]

Origen was a famous teacher and writer who flourished around the year 200. History admires him for making himself a eunuch (an act he later regretted), for prodigious learning, for composing the first systematic theology, and for bravely enduring imprisonment and torture for Christ. In his greatest work, *De Principiis*, he wrote about the angels -

> (Do not) suppose that it is the result of accident that a particular office is assigned to a particular angel: as for example to Raphael, the work of curing and healing; to Gabriel, the conduct of wars; to Michael, the duty of attending to the prayers and supplications of mortals. For we are not to imagine that they obtained these offices otherwise than by their own merits, and by the zeal and excellent qualities which they severally displayed before this world was formed; so that afterwards, in the order of archangels, this or that office was assigned to each one, while others deserved to be enrolled in the order of angels, and to act under this or that archangel, or that leader or head of an order ... (So) that to one angel the church of the Ephesians was to be entrusted; to another, that of the Smyrnaeans; one angel was to be Peter's, another Paul's; and so on through every one of the little ones that are in the church, for such and such angels as even daily behold the face of God must be assigned to each one of them; and there must also be some angel that encampeth round about them that fear God (Bk 1, ch 8).

---

[59]   Stromata, Bk 6, ch 17.

The same Origen, in his *Commentary on Matthew*, discusses Mt 18:10, and has some strange things to say: (1) he argues that the phrase little ones refers, not to children, but to new Christians; (2) he then debates whether these little ones have an angel appointed to guard them from the day of their natural birth, or only from the day of their supernatural birth; (3) he finds himself unable to resolve the matter, but he does suggest the following extraordinary solution-

> A third exposition of this passage might be something like the following, which would say, that as it is possible for a man to change from unbelief to faith, and from intemperance to temperance, and generally from wickedness to virtue, so also is it possible that the angel, to whom my soul has been entrusted at birth, may be wicked at the first, but afterwards may at some time believe in proportion as the man believes, and may make such advance that he may become one of the angels who always behold the face of the Father in heaven ... And it may be that as when a man and his wife are both unbelievers, sometimes it is the man who first believes and in time saves the wife, and sometimes the wife who begins and afterwards in time persuades her husband, so it happens with angels and men. If, however, anything of this kind takes place in the case of other angels or not, you may seek out for yourself. (par. 28)

But then,[60] Origen argues that we have these angels only while we are immature in the faith (that is, little ones), for as soon as we reach a place of strong faith we come under the direct guardianship of the Lord himself, and have no need of angelic intermediaries!

---

[60] The Old Testament Pseudepigrapha, Vol One, ed. J. H. Charlesworth; Doubleday & Co, New York; 1983; pg 896,897.

Anonymous -

> I said to the angel who was with me: "Has then each just person an angel for a companion?" And he said to me: "Each one of the saints has his own angel assisting him, and saying a hymn, and the one does not depart from the other" (The Vision of Paul, par. 49, c. 350).

2. THE PAIR OF ANGELS

Hermas began life as a slave, became a Christian, was freed, and made a fortune in trade (c. 130). He was an early John Bunyan, describing a holy life in the form of a visionary similitude. His book had an enormous influence, and many churches added it to their Bibles. He wrote -

> There are two angels with a man - one of righteousness, and the other of iniquity ... The angel of righteousness is gentle and modest, meek and peaceful ... When all these (virtues) ascend into your heart, know that the angel of righteousness is with you ... Look now at the works of the angel of iniquity. First, he is wrathful, and bitter, and foolish, and his works are evil, and ruin the servants of God ... When these ascend into your heart, know that the angel of iniquity is with you ... These, then, are the actions of both angels. Understand them, and trust the angel of righteousness; but depart from the angel of iniquity, because his instruction is bad in every deed (The Shepherd, Bk 2, Com 6, ch 2).

You may recall from the previous chapter, in popular belief it was thought that each person's righteous guardian angel bore a close resemblance to the person. I noted then that a reflection of that idea can be seen in Ac 12:14-15.

3. ANGELIC REPORTERS

An anonymous late 4th century work depicts angels assessing and reporting human deeds -

> *... bless God without ceasing, and yet more when the sun is setting. For at this hour all the angels come to God to adore him, and they bring before him the works of men, of each what he has done from morning to evening, whether good or evil. And one angel goes rejoicing on account of man when he behaves well, and another goes with a sad countenance ... (then follows a charming description of groups of cheerful angels coming with reports of good men) ... (But) when they went away, behold, there came other angels to worship God, mourning and weeping. And the Spirit went forth to meet them, and there came a voice to them: Whence have ye come? And they answered and said: We have come from those who have been called by thy name, and are slaves to the matter of sin. Why, then, is it necessary to minister to them? And there came a voice to them: Do not cease to minister to them; perhaps they will turn; but if not, they shall come to me, and I will judge them. Know then, sons of men, that all that is done by you day by day, the angels write in the heavens! (The Revelation of Paul, c. 380).*

The same idea is also presented, in almost the same terms, though not so vividly, in *The Vision of Paul,* par. 7, c. 350.

There is also a story of Michael going up in the evening from the tent of Abraham, to report about the patriarch to God, in The Testament of Abraham, probably written in Egypt by an anonymous scribe, c. 100 -

It came to pass, when the days of Abraham's death drew near, the Lord said to Michael, "Arise and go to Abraham my servant and say to him, You shall depart from life, because, behold, the days of your temporal life are fulfilled, so that he may administer the affairs of his household before he dies. And Michael went and came to Abraham ... And the sun was near setting. And Michael went outside the house, and he was taken up into the heavens to worship before God; for at the setting of the sun all angels worship God ... Michael answered before God and said, "Lord, command me to be questioned before your holy glory." And the Lord said to Michael, "Tell whatever you wish" ... The archangel answered and said, "Lord ... (Abraham) is your friend, and a righteous man, who welcomes strangers" ... Then Michael left for Abraham's house in that evening, and he found them preparing supper. And they ate, and drank, and made merry (Recension B, ch 1:1-3; 4:4-10; 5:1. The same story is told at greater length in Recension A).[61]

Clement of Alexandria (mentioned above) also believed an angel was examining and reporting his daily actions. Knowing a watching angel was beside one, he said, was a strong incentive not to sin! He spoke about the "intensely keen perception" of the angels, and reckoned sin could be hidden neither from them, nor from God. Thus, even in secret, the pious man will be strict in his observance of righteousness! (Stromata, Bk 7, ch 7).

---

[61] The above quotes from early Christian writings, where no other source is given, all come from The Ante-Nicene Fathers, in. loc.

4. ANGELS AND THE SOULS OF THE RIGHTEOUS

The *Revelation Of Paul*, mentioned above, tells how angels care for and gather the souls of both good and evil people -

> And I looked, and saw one of the sons of men falling near death. And the angel says to me: This is a righteous man, and, behold, all his works stand beside him in the hour of his necessity. And there were beside him good angels, and along with them also evil angels. And the evil angels indeed found no place in him, but the good took possession of the soul of the righteous man, and said to it: Take note of the body whence thou art coming out; for it is necessary for thee again to return to it in the day of resurrection, that thou mayest receive what God hath promised to the righteous ... (And that soul went with the good angels) and the Spirit came forth to meet them, saying: Come, soul, enter the place of the resurrection, which God hath prepared for his righteous ones ... (then follows a vivid description of the soul of an impious being seized by the evil angels, who cast it into darkness, while that soul's good angel ran beside it lamenting its doom and rebuking it for not heeding the angel's benign influence) ... (See also The Vision of Paul, par. 14).

5. ANGELS AND ASTROLOGY

Theodotus was probably a 3rd century Montanist. Only fragments of his writings remain, including the following -

> The stars, spiritual bodies, that have communications with the angels set over them, and are governed by them, are not the cause of the production of things, but are signs of what is taking

place, and will take place, and have taken place in the atmospheric changes, of fruitfulness and barrenness, of pestilence and fevers, and in the case of men. The stars do not in the least degree exert influences, but indicate what is, and will be, and has been (Excerpt # 55 from The Ante- Nicene Fathers, Vol 8; in loc.).

A similar idea, as I have mentioned earlier, seems to be reflected in Ro 8:38-39.

6. ANGELS AND PRAYER

In another work, Origen added to the ideas quoted above -

> ... (the angels) ascend, bearing the supplications of men, to the purest of the heavenly places in the universe ... and (then) they come down from these, conveying to each one, according to his deserts, something enjoined by God to be conferred by them upon those who are to be the recipients of his benefits (Contra Celsus, Bk 5, ch 4).

But he was adamant that no angel may be invoked in prayer -

> ... (never) are we commanded to honour and worship in place of God those who minister to us, and bear to us his blessings. For every prayer, and supplication, and intercession, and thanksgiving is to be sent up to the Supreme God through the High Priest, who is above all the angels, the Living Word and God (Ibid.) ... Moreover, as we know that it is not demons, but angels, who have been set over the fruits of the earth, and over the birth of animals, it is the latter that we praise and bless, as having been appointed by God over the things needful for our race; yet even to them we will not give the honour which is due to God. For this would not be pleasing

to God, nor would it be any pleasure to the angels themselves ... (Ibid. Bk 8, 57).

He goes on to tell how angels fight for us -

> ... when we have the favour of God, we have also the goodwill of all angels and spirits who are friends of God ... (The angels) co-operate with them in their endeavours to please God: they seek his favour on their behalf; with their prayers they join their own prayers ... We may indeed boldly say, that men who aspire after better things have, when they pray to God, tens of thousands of sacred powers upon their side ... And these, regarding all as their relations and friends who imitate their piety towards God ... visit with all manner of kindness and deliverance those who pray to God ... We do not, then, deny that there are many demons upon earth, but we maintain that they exist and exercise power among the wicked, as a punishment of their wickedness. But they have no power over those who have "put on the whole armour of God" (and) who have received strength to withstand "the wiles of the devil" ... (Ibid. ch 64, 34, 35)

B. WHAT DOES THE BIBLE SAY?

How much does scripture support those early Christian ideas about guardian angels?

1. ANGELS DO HELP US

Without doubt, angels are commissioned to guard the servants of God. Thus the intervention of an angel prevented Abraham from killing Isaac (Ge 22:11), and Abraham's servant testified that the angel of God had travelled with him (24:40). Jacob sang that an angel of God had redeemed him from all evil, and he was sure the same angel would bless the sons of Joseph (48:16). God promised Moses and Israel his angel would go before them to *"guard you on the way and to bring you to the place which I have prepared"* (Ex 23:20-23).

Several hundred years later, Elisha was quietly confident the angels of God were still defending Israel. His servant was not so sure, so Elisha prayed, *"O Lord, open his eyes that he may see."* So the Lord opened the eyes of the young man, and *"behold, the mountain was full of horses and chariots of fire"* (2 Kg 6:16-17). But he should not have needed such a vision, for scripture already contained the promise: *"The angel of the Lord encamps around those who fear him, and delivers them"* (Ps 34:7); and again: *"He will give his angels charge of you to guard you in all your ways"* (91:11).

Even during the exile, the true people of God expressed confidence in the continuing protection of their guardian angels (cp. Da 3:25; 6:22). An angel who spoke to Daniel said that he, at least for a time, was the guardian of Darius, while the archangel Michael was at least temporarily Daniel's *"prince"* (Da 11:1; 10:21). Michael, however, may have been the guardian of Daniel only in the broader sense of being *"prince"* over all Israel.

So beyond personal protection, the scriptures do speak about angels whom God has appointed to guard, or control, whole nations (Da 10:13-11:1). Perhaps also cities, churches, and other entities may have guardian angels (cp. Re 1:20; 2:1; etc). There are also angels associated with fire (Re 14:18), wind (Re 7:1; and cp. Ps 104:4); and water (Re 16:3-5).

2. ARE THEY ASSIGNED TO US?

None of those passages, however, is definite enough to support the idea that every person, or even every godly person, has a particular guardian angel. There is no support for the myth that we each have two angels linked with us, and that the good angel resembles the person he guards. The most I can say from the evidence gathered so far is this: the angels of God do guard the people of God; and God may sometimes instruct a single angel to guide and protect one of his servants. But you need not conclude that a particular angel is constantly attending every Christian.

3. GUARDIANS OF CHILDREN?

One passage remains: "See that you do not despise one of these little ones; for I tell you that in heaven their angels always behold the face of my Father who is in heaven" (Mt 18:10).

From that passage people have often supposed every person does have a guardian angel. Some commentators have thought the same. William Barclay suggests Jesus was here reflecting, perhaps even endorsing, popular Jewish (and later Christian) views -

> In the time of Jesus the Jews believed in a very highly- developed angelology. Every nation had its angel; every natural force, such as the wind and the thunder and the lightning and the rain had its angel. They even went the length of saying very beautifully that every blade of grass has its angel. So, then, they believed that every child has his guardian angel. Further, to say that these angels behold the face of God in heaven means that these angels also have a right of direct access to God. The picture is the picture of a great royal court where only the most favoured courtiers and ministers and officials have direct access to the king. In the sight of God the children are so important that their guardian angels always have the right of direct access to the inner presence of God.[62]

---

[62] The Daily Study Bible, Vol 2, *Gospel of Matthew*; The Saint Andrew Press, Edinburgh; 1965; pg 199.

Other commentators suggest that Christ was referring to the Jewish notion that every person has a heavenly counterpart, a kind of "spiritual double", who always has access to the Father's presence. That idea too was taken up with some enthusiasm by the early Christians. For example, a 4th century document, The Testament Of Our Lord, spoke about all men having "figures of their souls, which stand before the Father of Light." But if a person is ungodly, then his spiritual double will share his doom, and will "perish, and (be) carried to darkness to dwell."

However, one aspect of Christ's saying seems to preclude the thought of every one of God's children having a guardian angel. He said, *"Their angels always behold the face of my Father who is in heaven."* Does that mean angels can be on earth guarding the saints, while standing before the throne of God in heaven? If not, what is the sense of Jesus' words?

The *"little ones"* he speaks of are certainly children, but not exclusively so; for by a common usage of the time, Jesus probably intended *"little ones"* to include his disciples, that is, those who believe him, whatever their age may be (cp. vs. 4,6,14). And you should probably give the phrase *"their angels"* the same meaning as He 1:14. That is, all the holy angels are "our" angels (better, "my" angels), because God has commissioned them to the task of ministering to the heirs of salvation.

Therefore the words of Jesus should be given a broad rather than a narrow meaning. He was saying that these same angels, who serve all the children of God, also have access to the immediate presence of God. The saints have friends in the royal court! Their ministers stand before the Monarch of the universe! They have great and powerful allies! So beware how you speak of them and behave towards them!

No wonder Christ added: *"See that you do not despise one of these little ones"* - lest you antagonise the Almighty and the glorious angels who stand in his presence.

4. NO PARTICULAR ANGEL

So I do not think of myself as having a particular guardian angel, constantly attending me, bearing my likeness and involved in my daily life. Rather, I acknowledge that from the shining hosts who stand in his presence the Father may at any time dispatch for my succour either a single angel or a glittering squadron, and that these swift armies are eager to do his bidding, and to minister to me, an heir of salvation.

Thus Jesus did not claim any one angel as his peculiar guardian; but he did say that on his request the Father would send him twelve legions of angels (Mt 26:53); and we read of one occasion when a group of angels ministered to him (Mt 4:11; Mk 1:13); and of another occasion when a single angel ministered to him (Lu 22:43).

5. AN IMPLAUSIBLE DOCTRINE?

Some people have resisted the idea of angelic succour of any kind. They argue that the doctrine is implausible by any measure. Something so improbable, so far removed from ordinary experience, they say, must be suspect. Albert Barnes gives a fine reply -

> In this doctrine there is nothing absurd. It is no more improbable that angels should be employed to aid man, than that one man should aid another; certainly not as improbable as that the Son of God should come down, *"not to be ministered unto, but to minister"* (Mt 20:28), and that he performed on earth the office of a servant (Jn 13:1-15). Indeed, it is a great principle of the Divine administration, that one class of God's creatures are to minister to others; that one is to aid another - to assist him in trouble, to provide for him when poor, and to counsel him in perplexity. We are constantly deriving benefit from others, and are dependent

upon their counsel and help. Thus, God has appointed parents to aid their children; neighbours to aid their neighbours; the rich to aid the poor; and all over the world the principle is seen, that one is to derive benefit from the aid of others.

Why may not the angels be employed in this service?

They are pure, benevolent, powerful; and as man was ruined in the fall by the temptation offered by one of an angelic, though fallen nature, why should not others of angelic unfallen holiness, come to assist in repairing the evils which their fallen, guilty brethren have inflicted on the race?

To me there seems to be a beautiful propriety in bringing aid from another race, as ruin came from another race; and that as those endowed with angelic might, though with fiendish malignity, ruined man, those with angelic might, but heavenly benevolence, should aid in his recovery and salvation.[63]

In brief, as surely as fallen angels roam at large, seeking to harm the kingdom of God, it is comforting to know that many more good angels swiftly fly, powerful to establish the kingdom of God!

II. HOW THE ANGELS HELP US

Angels serve the heirs of salvation in several striking ways -

---

[63] Exactly the same Greek word is used in both places, and in the Greek (LXX) text of Leviticus, *mnemosunon*.

A. BY PHYSICAL ACTION

Angels are spirit-beings, yet they are able to exert physical power; they can influence, change, or control the material world. You cannot restrict angels to specifically "spiritual" forms of behaviour.

Hence we read about angels: touching people; providing food and drink; calling down fire from heaven; pursuing and destroying God's enemies; protecting people from fire and from wild animals; killing by pestilence, on one occasion, some 70,000 people, and on another 185,000; causing earthquakes; moving great stones; releasing people from prison; breaking iron fetters; and the like (Nu 20:16; 2 Sa 24:16; 2 Kg 19:35; Ps 35:5; 91:11; Da 6:22; Mt 4:11; 28:2; Mk 1:13; Ac 5:19; 12:7)

B. BY SPIRITUAL INFLUENCE

1. BEYOND PHYSICAL SUSTENANCE

Angels are able to provide people with inner spiritual renewal, to fortify human courage, to strengthen the will, to quicken spiritual perception; and the like (Lu 22:43; Da 10:17; Ez 8:1-4; etc.)

However, I believe they cannot gain access to the human mind or spirit against the will of the person concerned. The mind is inviolate against unbidden intrusion, except by the Spirit of God who knows the innermost secrets of every heart. The angels may know nothing of my thoughts unless I choose to disclose them.

2. THE ANGELS ARE ALSO HELPERS OF OUR WORSHIP

Another angel came and stood at the altar with a golden censer, and he was given much incense to mingle with the prayers of all the saints upon the golden altar before the throne; and the smoke of the incense rose with the prayers of the saints from the hand of the angel before God (Re 8:3-4).

While some angels are busy in heaven adding a sweet fragrance to the sound of our worship before it reaches the throne of God, others are joining their praises with those of the saints on earth.

Paul says that because of the presence of the angels in church *"a woman ought to have a veil on her head"* (1 Co. 11:10). Commentators differ in their understanding of that rather obscure statement. Some suggest it means women should wear a veil because of the clergy who are present, or as a protection against the fallen angels, or because the angels in heaven veil themselves in the presence of God.

Others suggest it reflects Paul's belief that angels gather with the saints in worship, and that in deference to these glorious, if unseen, visitors, women should remain veiled. Such an argument may not seem impressive to modern daughters of God, who steadfastly (and I think rightly) refuse to wear veils to church - but the point can still be taken that angels are present when the people of God gather in worship.

David apparently recognised this when he sang: *"I give thee thanks, O Lord, with my whole heart; before the gods (angels) I sing thy praise"* (Ps 138:1).

C. AS MESSENGERS

1. FROM HEAVEN TO EARTH

More often than any other activity, and in character with the meaning of their name, angels bear the title and task of messenger. This courier work takes many shapes:

- ◆ warning of danger, guiding to safety: Ge 18 and 19; Ac 12:6-11; 27:21-25.

- predicting the future: Jg 13:3-5; Da 8:19; 12:6-7; Lu 1:11-19, 26-35; Re 1:1.

- giving wisdom and understanding: Da 9:23; Lu 24:4-9.

- giving instruction and direction: Mt 1:20; 2:13, 19- 20; 28:5-7; Mk 16:5-7; Ac 8:26; 10:3-6,22.

- explaining the nature of certain events: Mt 28:5; Mk 16:5-6; Lu 2:9-14.

- giving a commission to serve God: Jg 6:12-14; Ac 5:19-20; 7:35-38.

- interpreting visions: Da 7:16; 8:16-17; Zc 1:9,19; Re 17:7.

Scripture shows that angels use two main methods in their task of communicating to man the words of God:

- dreams, Ge 31:11; Mt 1:20; 2:13,19

- direct encounter, Jg 6:11; etc.

How active are the angels today in that ministry? If you require visibility, or recognition, they would seem to be almost wholly inactive. Yet they may be communicating much more than we know, for the success of their work does not depend upon human perception. Perhaps if God opened our eyes (as he did for Elisha's young servant) our astonishment at what the angels are saying and doing would be overwhelming!

2. FROM EARTH TO HEAVEN

Our vows are heard betimes!
And heaven takes care
To grant, before we can conclude the prayer:
Preventing angels met it half the way,
And sent us back to praise,
Who came to pray!
- John Dryden, *Britannia Rediviva* (1688)

Does scripture support the poet's suggestion that angels are somehow connected with our prayers? Yes, if not always, at least sometimes, they carry our petitions to the Father's throne. For example, Eliphaz insisted no sinner can expect an angel to intercede for him -

> *Call now; is there any one who will answer you? To which of the holy ones will you turn? (Jb 5:1).*

The question would be pointless unless Eliphaz and his friends believed angels had a part to play in intercessory prayer. The picture is one of an oriental palace, where a prince is pleading with a monarch to be gracious to a humble client.

Elihu describes a similar scene. An angel stands by a sick man, presenting God with reasons to heal him -

> *Yet if an angel, one of thousands, stands by him, a mediator between him and God, to expound what he has done right and to secure mortal man his due; if he speaks in the man's favour and says, "Reprieve him, let him not go down to the pit, I have the price of his release;" then that man will grow sturdier than when he was in youth, he will return to the days of his prime. (Jb 33:23-25, NEB)*

Elihu reckoned any person who gains such angelic support will find his prayer made wonderfully powerful! He can expect God to answer with a mighty miracle. If he is sick, he will win much more than a cure - the Lord will restore his very youth!

Zechariah gives an even clearer picture of angelic intercession -

> *Then the angel of the Lord said, "O Lord of hosts, how long wilt thou have no mercy on Jerusalem and the cities of Judah, against which thou hast had indignation these seventy years?" And the Lord answered gracious and comforting words to the angel who talked with me (1:12).*

Notice how the angel lacked full knowledge of the purpose of God, yet was free to approach the throne on behalf of Israel, and there receive a pleasant answer from the Lord. The prophet saw the angel behaving much as a man would.

The scene is still more vivid in the apocryphal book of Tobit, where Raphael says -

> When you and Sarah prayed, it was I who brought your prayers into the glorious presence of the Lord ... God sent me to cure both you and Sarah your daughter-in-law at the same time. I am Raphael, one of the seven angels who stand in attendance on the Lord and enter his glorious presence (12:12-15; NEB).

Raphael not only carried Tobit's prayers to God, he also returned to Tobit with a miracle of healing. That passage may not be scripture; but Luke tells about another angel whose behaviour was similar (Ac 10:1-8). Notice how the angel commended Cornelius' prayers, and brought him an answer and a message from God.

Both passages associate prayer with the *"memorial sacrifice"* commanded by Moses (Le 2:2,9,16). Just as the ancient priest took an offering from the hand of a worshipper, and burned it on the altar as *"a pleasing odour to the Lord"*, so the two angels presented the prayers of their wards: Raphael presented Tobit's prayer as *"a memorial before the Holy One"* (Tb 12:12); and the other angel said to Cornelius, *"Your prayers and your alms have ascended as a memorial before God"* (Ac 10:4).[64] There is a striking similarity in wording. The first story may be fiction, and the second history, but they share a common idea about the participation of the angels in our prayers.

---

[64] James Inglis, Notes on the Book of Genesis; Gall and Inglis, Edinburgh/London, 1877; pg 260.

Am I saying you cannot pray effectively without angelic support? Of course not! Does this mean the mediation of Christ is inadequate, and we need further intervention by angels? Hardly! What could any angel add to the perfect intercessory ministry of our great High Priest? (He 7:25; etc.)

Yet it pleases the Lord to give useful work to his servants. We know that whatever he does he could do unaided. But he delights to gladden his faithful ones, angelic and human, by making them partners with him in building his kingdom. Thus it seems God has appointed a role for angels in conveying our prayers to heaven and in creating his answer on earth.

Nonetheless, your focus must never be on the messenger, no matter how heavenly or tic, but on the King. He alone deserves your worship and your trust.

D. AS MEDIATORS OF THE LAW

The record in Exodus (19:16-25) says nothing about the presence of angels on Mt. Sinai, and we are left with an impression that the Lord God stood alone upon the mountain with Moses. But later, Moses himself associated angels with Sinai; and still later, the psalmist was even more emphatic -

> *The Lord came from Sinai ... he came from the ten thousands of the holy ones, with flaming fire at his right hand ... With mighty chariotry, twice ten thousand, thousands upon thousands, the Lord came from Sinai into the holy place (De 33:2; Ps 68:17).*

The Jews strengthened such references into a firm tradition that the law had been given to Moses by the mediation of angels, and the early church readily accepted that idea (Ac 7:53; Ga 3:19; He 2:2). This giving of the law to Moses by the hands of angels, said the rabbis, covered it with a peculiar glory. Who could doubt that the touch of angels brought to the law an incomparable lustre?

But the apostles argued differently. They contended that the gospel was incomparably superior to the law. Why? Because the gospel came, not by the agency of created beings, but by the hand of the eternal Son. Angels may stand between the law and God; but who dares to interpose anything between the gospel and God? (Ga 3:19-26; He 1 and 2).

The ministry of angels may be glorious; but the ministry of the Son is exceedingly glorious! Let no angel therefore ever stand between you and Christ, nor turn you aside from the free and perfect access into the holiest God has given you in Christ. (Ga 1:6-8; He 10:19-23).

E. BY WARRING AGAINST EVIL

Heaven and earth are today both battlegrounds in which Michael and his angels are warring against Satan and his angels. This battle continues relentlessly, and will do so until Christ returns. It is interesting to speculate how much evil there would be in the world if the powers of darkness could defeat the holy angels. Even now the wickedness and suffering of the human race seems almost immeasurable; but how much worse might it be if the armies of God were not restraining the devil and his hordes?

However, there is no risk of the holy angels suffering defeat. After all, God has been content to commit only part of their number to this combat with the fallen angels! Sometimes the struggle becomes an individual one in which the enemy may press hard upon an angel of God. But defeat is still impossible, for God's champion has great reserves upon which to draw! (cp. Da 10:12-13,20-21).

One day Christ will call into battle Michael and all the holy angels, and on that day the overthrow of the satanic hordes will be instant and complete. Christ will overthrow and ruin them for ever (Re 19:11-20:10).

Did you notice how John placed a number on the denizens of darkness - he saw them counted as 200 million (Re 9:16)? But the number of the celestial cohorts is immeasurable: *"myriads of myriads, and thousands of thousands"* (Re 5:11). I suppose those numbers are figurative; but they still convey a stunning image of a finite number of demons matched against an almost infinite array of angels. We need have no fear of the kingdom of darkness extinguishing the glory of heaven!

The trumpet of war sounds in many places in the Bible. Scripture calls angels the *"army"* of God, and God is The Lord of Hosts -

> *And (the angel) said, "No; but as commander of the army of the Lord I have now come (Js 5:14).*

> *Lord God of Hosts (1 Sa 1:3,11; 1 Kg 22:19; Ps 24:10; 46:7,11; Ho 12:5; Am 3:13; 6:14).*

Then there is that peculiar incident in the life of Jacob -

> *Jacob went on his way, and the angels of God met him; and when Jacob saw them he said, "This is God's army!" So he called the name of that place "Mahanaim" (Ge 32:1-2).*

Inglis explains it this way -

> This appears to have been a waking vision ... (The army) was God's host, and sent by him for (Jacob's) protection. In the vision at Bethel the angels of God appear as messengers ascending and descending; here they are an army of defence. "Mahanaim" is the dual (or plural) of the word rendered army and signifies two armies (Ca 6:13). He calls the angels an army, on account of their number, and of the manner in which they appeared on his behalf; and

he calls the place "Mahanaim", "two armies", because they consisted of two bands. At Bethel also there were two bands - angels ascending and descending. There, as suited his spiritual necessities, they were meant to lift his thoughts above the earth to heaven; here, as he is in danger, they are an army for his protection (Ps 34:7).[65]

By contrast, Keil and Delitzsch comment -

When Laban had taken his departure peaceably, Jacob pursued his journey to Canaan. He was then met by some angels of God, in whom he discerned an encampment of God; and he called the place where they appeared "Mahanaim", that is, double camp, or double host, because the host of God joined his host as a safeguard. This appearance of angels necessarily reminded him of the vision of the ladder, on his flight from Canaan. Just as the angels ascending and descending had then represented to him divine protection and assistance during his journey and sojourn in a foreign land, so now the angelic host was a signal of the help of God for the approaching conflict with Esau of which he was in fear, and a fresh pledge of the promise (38:15), "I will bring thee back to the land," etc. Jacob saw it during his journey; in a waking condition, therefore, not internally, but out of or above himself: but whether with the eye of the body or of the mind (cp. 2 Kg 6:17) cannot be determined.[66]

---

[65] Commentary on the Old Testament, The Pentateuch, pg 301; William B, Eerdmans Pub. Co., Grand Rapids, Michigan; 1976 reprint. Emphasis mine.

[66] Tyndale Old Testament Commentaries, Genesis, pg 167; The Tyndale Press, London, UK, 1968. Emphasis mine.

Derek Kidner notes that Jacob saw this camp of militant angels while he was *"on his way"* - that is, returning to Canaan in obedience to the command of God. The spiritual lesson is that -

> reassurance was given as he went forward (cf. Lu 17:14; Jn 4:51), and what came to meet him out of the unknown was God's host (cp. Is 64:5), a reminder and new foretaste of Bethel. The force of the name Mahanaim ("double camp"), is that another company, as Jacob could see, now marched with his own. It was a heartening beginning to his ordeal, in which very soon his own company would be split up for fear of a massacre (vs. 8).[67]

> Whether Jacob's exclamation *"Mahanaim!"* means there is one full company of angels to match each group of the people of God, or that there are two companies of angels ready to defend every servant of God, the idea is the same: those who are on our side are more numerous and powerful than our foe!

John saw an awesome vision of the armies of heaven campaigning against evil (Re 19:14), and Jude remembered that even old Enoch had understood this spiritual reality: *"Behold, the Lord came with his holy myriads, to execute judgment on all"* (vs. 14-15).

These things are spoken to reassure us, so that we may exult in the inevitable triumph that lies before us.

F. AS OUR COMPANIONS AT DEATH

Thomas Ady, in 1656, gave us the earliest written version of the ancient children's evening prayer -

> Matthew, Mark, Luke, and John,

---

[67]   Hastings, op. cit., Vol 1, pg 57.

The Bed be blest that I lie on.
Four angels to my bed,
Four angels round my head,
One to watch, and one to pray,
And two to bear my soul away.

The song expresses the simple idea that should the child die during the night, he would not die alone. Angels were there throughout the dark hours to protect him, or, if God should so will, to carry him safely to heaven.

The Bible suggests the same. We read that Lazarus, when he died, *"was carried by the angels to Abraham's bosom"* (Lu 16:22).

> We come here upon a widespread belief among Jews and Jewish Christians - that angels convey the souls of the righteous to Paradise. Michael is usually the one entrusted with this duty. If he has a companion, it is Gabriel. The Gospel of Nicodemus records that when Jesus descended into Hades and released the righteous dead from captivity, he delivered Adam and all the righteous to the Archangel Michael, and all the saints followed Michael; and he led them all into the glorious gate of Paradise: among them being the penitent thief. The History of Joseph the Carpenter records that Michael and Gabriel drew out the soul of Joseph and wrapped it in a silken napkin, and amid the songs of angels took him to his good Father, even to the dwelling-place of the just. In the Testament of Abraham we have a similar account of the death of Abraham. The Ascension of Isaiah (7:25) affirms that "those who love the Most High and his Beloved

will ascend to heaven by the Angel of the Holy
Spirit."[68]

G. BY GATHERING US TO CHRIST ON THE LAST DAY

The last, the greatest, the most splendid service the angels will
render the church on earth, will be to call all the saints of all time
together on the day of resurrection, and to present them glorious to
Christ -

> *Then will appear the sign of the Son of man in
> heaven, and then all the tribes of the earth will
> mourn, and they will see the Son of man coming on
> the clouds of heaven with power and great glory;
> and he will send out his angels with a loud trumpet
> call, and they will gather his elect from the four
> winds, from one end of heaven to the other (Mt
> 24:30-31; see also Mk 13:27; 1 Th 4:16-18; 2 Th
> 2:1).*

May the Lord hasten the coming of that glad hour!

CONCLUSION

I have not said all there is to say about the angels; nor can I claim
that what I have said is absolutely reliable. Angelology involves
speculation; and while I have striven to keep conjecture to a
minimum, it still exists, and it may be wrong. You will have to
determine for yourself how truly I have written, and how well these
pages reflect the teaching of scripture. I hope I have not strayed too
far (if at all) from the revelation of God.

---

[68] Victory Pageant - a commentary on the *Book of Revelation*, pg 30; Pickering and
Inglis Ltd., London, 1972

Belief in angels remains a fascinating theory unless one has had a tangible angelic encounter. I have not yet had such an experience. Does that mean angels have not been active in my life? No, only that I have not consciously seen or felt them. I do not doubt they have been active, but I have no way of identifying that activity.

Those many answers to prayer I have had - were they wrought by angels, or by the direct hand of God? Those many times I was saved from serious accident and injury - did the Lord deliver me himself, or by the mediacy of angels? Perhaps sometimes angels were there, perhaps every time. I cannot tell.

But I believe in the angels. And I am grateful that this belief gives me a deeper insight, both into my own existence as a man, and into the splendours of God's government and kingdom. I look forward with eager pleasure to the day when all the sons of God, angels and men, will be openly revealed to the whole creation.

So let me conclude by suggesting three special benefits that come to us from the doctrine of angels -

♦ just as we learn most other things by contrasting one against another, so we gain a better understanding of our own humanity and of our place in the scheme of things by measuring ourselves against the angels;

♦ the glory of the cross is enhanced by recognising that even the mightiest of angels have a vested interest in our salvation; without us, they remain diminished;

♦ we gain a glimpse behind the veil, to perceive the spiritual realm that exists all around us, and with whose destiny ours is inextricably bound.

ADDENDA

A. TITLES AND NAMES

Here is a list of the various titles by which the angels are identified in scripture -

◆ *Mahanaim* ("Two camps") - Ge 32:1-2

◆ *God's Hosts* - Ps 103:21

◆ *God's Ministers* - Ps 103:21

◆ *Elohim (or "gods')* - Ge 35:7; Ps 8:5; 138:1

◆ *Holy Ones* - De 33:2; Jb 5:1

◆ *Saints* - Ps 89:5,7

◆ *Sons of God* - Jb 1:6; 2:1

◆ *Watchers* - Da 4:13; Is 62:2

◆ *Angels of Light (contra the angels of darkness)* 2 Co 11:14; Ep 6:12

◆ *Princes* - Da 10:13; 12:1

◆ *Spirits* - He 1:14

◆ *The Armies of Heaven* - Re 19:14

◆ *The Destroyer* - 1 Co 10:10. The reference is to Nu 16:46-49, where no angel is mentioned; but Ex 12:23; 2 Sa 24:16.

B. "THE ANGELS OF THE SEVEN CHURCHES"

See Re 1:20; 2:1,8,12,18; 3:1,7,14.

The four commonest explanations of the identity of these "angels" of the churches are -

1. "Angel" here carries its literal sense of "messenger", and the reference is to the "postmen" chosen by John to deliver his letters to the seven churches. However, there is no evidence that the seven letters were circulated separately, and it is more probable that they always were what they are now, an integral part of the whole book. Furthermore, John was not told to send letters "by" these "messengers", but "to" them.

2. Since all other 67 occurrences of angelos in the Apocalypse clearly refer to actual angels, it is reasonable to suppose that in these 8 references the word has the same meaning. So it should be taken as referring to the "guardian angel" of each church. However, there is no other clear statement in scripture that churches do have permanent angelic guardians. In any case, it is strange behaviour to write letters to angels, particularly when those letters contain accusations of spiritual failure and of sin. So it seems improbable that John was writing to real angels.

3. "Angel" should be seen as a figurative way of describing the bishop, pastor, or senior minister of each church. This is a more plausible interpretation, yet it has a weakness. There is no other evidence that so early in the history of the church the practice had been adopted of appointing one man to a position of dominance in each congregation or district. On the contrary, it is more probable that the plural eldership mentioned in Ph 1:1 (etc) was still the common practice. Even if the churches did so early have individual pastors and/or bishops, why call them "angels"?

4. Possibly the best explanation is that offered by R. S. Orr, in common with several other commentators -

> Only twenty years or so had passed since Paul had spoken the words of Ac 20:28, "Take heed to yourselves and to all the flock, in which the Holy Spirit has made you guardians." If a similar body of men was held responsible for the church of Ephesus in John's day as in Paul's, then that body was the

council of local elders. We therefore consider the "angel" to be symbolic of the local elders acting together. In the NT, elders of the local church (or, to give them their alternative names, overseers, guardians, or bishops) are always referred to in the plural (Ac 14:23; 20:28; Ph 1:1; 1 Ti 5:17; Tit 1:5; Ja 5:14). The elders of each church are together viewed as a star (20), symbolising their unity and their heavenly ordination.[69]

So the Ephesian elders to whom Paul spoke, and the *"angel"* of the church at Ephesus to whom John wrote, may be seen as having a common identity.

C. "THE ANGEL OF THE LORD"

This expression occurs in both Testaments. However, while in the NT it seems to refer only to an angel fulfilling a particular task, in the OT it seems to have a much more profound meaning. Many commentators feel that in the OT *"the Angel of the Lord"* is none other than Christ, or a manifestation of the Deity. Technically, such a manifestation is called a theophany. What that means is discussed in my book *Emmanuel.*

---

[69] Notes on the New Testament; Kregel Publications, Grand Rapids, Michigan; 1966 reprint; pg 1231.

BIBLIOGRAPHY

Ante-Nicene Fathers, The; Eerdman's Pub. Co., Grand Rapids, Michigan; 1979.

Antiquities of the Jews; Josephus (70 A.D)

Believer's Bible Commentary; William Macdonald; Thomas Nelson Publishers; 1989.

Bible Background Commentary; Intervarsity Press; Nottingham, UK; 1993.

Bible Knowledge Commentary, The; by John Walvoord and Roy Zuck; Cook Communications, Colorado Springs, Colorado; 1989.

Calvin's Commentaries; John Calvin (1509-1564).

Church History; *Eusebius;* tr. C. F. Cruse; Baker Book House; 1977.

College Press NIV Commentary, The; Joplin, Missouri; 1996.

Commentary on Ephesians, A; Charles Hodge (1797-1878).

Commentary on the Bible; Adam Clarke (1715-1832).

Commentary On The Old And New Testaments, A; John Trapp (1601-1669).

Commentary on the Old and New Testaments, A; Robert Jamieson, A. R. Fausset, David Brown; 1871.

Commentary on the Old Testament; *The Pentateuch*; B. William; Eerdmans Pub. Co., Grand Rapids, Michigan; 1976 reprint.

Complete English Poems, The; John Donne; ed. A. J. Smith; Penguin Books; 1982.

Daily Study Bible, The; *Gospel of Matthew*; The Saint Andrew Press, Edinburgh; 1965.

Dictionary of Christ and the Gospels; ed. by James Hastings; *Angels*; Baker Book House, Grand Rapids, Michigan; 1973.

Dictionary Of Christian Lore And Legend, ed. J. C. J. Metford; Thames & Hudson, London; 1983.

Dictionary of Philosophy and Religion; ed. W. L. Reeses; Humanities Press, NJ; 1980.

Explanatory Notes on the Whole Bible; John Wesley (1703-1791).

Exposition of the Entire Bible; John Gill (1690-1771).

Expositor's Bible Commentary, The; ed. Frank E. Gaebelein; Zondervan Publishers; Grand Rapids, Michigan.

Expository Commentary; H. A. Ironside (1876-1951).

Facts On File Dictionary Of Religions; ed. John R. Hinnels; Facts On File Inc., New York; 1984; article *Merkabah Mysticism.*

Holman New Testament Commentary; ed. Max Anders; B & H Pub. Group, Nashville, Tennessee; 2004.

Holy Sonnets, John Donne, first printed in 1633.

International History Magazine, Editions Horizons, Lausanne, Switzerland; Sept. 1973.

Interpreter's Bible, The; Abingdon Press, New York; 1952.

IVP New Testament Commentary Series, The; Intervarsity Press, Nottingham, UK.

Jewish New Testament Commentary; David H. Stern; Jewish New Testament Publications, Inc., Clarksville, Maryland; 1982.

Koran Interpreted, The; *Sura 2;* tr. Arthur J Arberry; Oxford University Press, Oxford. UK.; 1964.

Koran, The, tr. N. J. Dawood; Penguin Books, London; 1980.

Matthew Henry's Commentary; Marshall, Morgan, and Scott, London; 1953.

Matthew Poole's Commentary; 1685

Nelson's New Illustrated Bible Commentary; Thomas Nelson Inc., New York; 1999.

New International Dictionary of the Christian Church, The; ed. J. D. Douglas; Paternoster Press, Exeter, UK; 1974; art. *Angels.*

New Testament Commentary; Baker's Publishing House, Grand Rapids, Michigan; 1987.

Nicene and Post-Nicene Fathers, The; Second Series, Volume One, *Eusebius*; Eerdman's Pub. Co., Grand Rapids, Michigan; 1979.

Notes on the Bible; Albert Barnes (1798-1870).

Notes on the Book of Genesis; James Inglis; Gall and Inglis, Edinburgh/London; 1877.

Notes on the New Testament; Kregel Publications, Grand Rapids, Michigan; 1966 reprint.

Old Testament Pseudepigrapha, The; *The Apocalypse of Enoch;* ed. J. H. Charlesworth; Doubleday & Co., New York; 1985.

Outlines of Theology; Eerdman's Pub. Co., Grand Rapids, Michigan, 1949.

People's New Testament Commentary, The; B. W. Johnson; Word Search Corporation, Nashville, Tennessee; 2010.

People's New Testament, The; B. W. Johnson; 1891.

Poor Man's Commentary On The Whole Bible, The; Robert Hawker; 1850.

Preacher's Commentary, The; Word Inc., Nashville, Tennessee; 1992.

Preacher's Outline and Sermon Bible; Word Search Corporation, Nashville, Tennessee; 2010.

Protevangelium of James,The; Anonymous; from Roberts and Donaldson.

Pulpit Commentary, The; ed. Joseph S. Exell, Henry Donald Maurice Spence-Jones; 1881.

Sirach; OT Apocrypha

Summa Theologicae, I.4.50.4.Basic Writings of Saint Thomas Aquinas, Vol. One; ed. Anton C. Pegis; Random House, New York; 1945; in. loc.

Systematic Theology, Pickering & Inglis Ltd., London, 1907.

Tobit; OT Apocrypha

Treasury of David; Vol 2; Zondervan Publishing House, Grand Rapids, Michigan; 1974 reprint.

Tyndale Old Testament Commentaries, *Genesis*, Tyndale Press; London, UK; 1968.

Victory Pageant, A Commentary; *The Book of Revelation*; Pickering and Inglis Ltd., London, 1972.

Vincent's Word Studies; Marvin R. Vincent; 1886

Week On The Concord And Merrimack Rivers, A; Henry David Thoreau; The Heritage Press, Norwalk, CT; 1975.

What Luther Says; compiled by E. W. Plass; Concordia Pub. House; St Louis, Missouri; 1959.

Wiersbe's Expository Outlines; Warren W. Wiersbe; Pub. David C. Cook; Colorado Springs, Colorado.

Word Pictures In The New Testament; A. T. Robertson; 1933.

www.ingramcontent.com/pod-product-compliance
Lightning Source LLC
Chambersburg PA
CBHW070758100426
42742CB00012B/2180